Frank has become one of today's leading Christian thinkers. *Shattered* is the story of how God worked in his life—the book will not only inspire and entertain, but it will also challenge each of us to grow in our own walk with God.

—DAVID BARTON

Founder and President, Wallbuilders

Shattered tells Frank Pastore's amazing story of going from being a pro baseball player and an atheist to becoming a fearless apologist and defender of the faith. Frank has a gift for taking the complex and making it understandable. He speaks and writes with passion. One of the best definitions of good communication is logic on fire. That is what Frank Pastore communicates, with great impact.

—GREG LAURIE

Senior Pastor, Harvest Christian Fellowship

Whether or not you were a fan of the Big Red Machine as I was growing up in Cincinnati, you'll be inspired by Frank's story. His purpose in life was not found on the mound of success and stardom, but in the valley of disappointment and despair. You'll find yourself laughing and crying (so don't read *Shattered* in public) as you walk with Frank in his discovery of life's greatest treasures: faith and family.

—TONY PERKINS

President, Family Research Council

Frank and Gina have it all, talent *and* treasure. But add one more T . . . trouble. *Lots* of it. Yet it's what makes their story so convincing and compelling. So *believable*. You may never have pitched in the

Major Leagues, ™ but here's a guy with whom you'll genuinely identify. It's great reading and *great* inspiration!

—JONI EARECKSON TADA
Joni and Friends International Disability Center

Frank Pastore is not just the energetic host of a major syndicated radio show. But he is a complete testimony of the work of God. *Shattered* tells of Frank's compelling journey through pain and recovery to healing and wholeness in Jesus. It's a great read.

—DR. CARL A. MOELLER
President and CEO, Open Doors USA

SHATTERED

STRUCK DOWN, BUT NOT DESTROYED

★ ★ ★

FRANK PASTORE

WITH ELLEN VAUGHN

Tyndale House Publishers, Inc.
Carol Stream, Illinois

A Focus on the Family book published by
Tyndale House Publishers, Inc., Carol Stream, Illinois 60188

Focus on the Family and the accompanying logo and design are federally
registered trademarks of Focus on the Family, Colorado Springs, CO
80995.

TYNDALE and Tyndale's quill logo are registered trademarks of Tyndale
House Publishers, Inc.

The author is represented by the literary agency of Wolgemuth & Associates.

Editor: Marianne Hering
Cover design by Erik M. Peterson
Back cover and page 1 of color insert: Major League Baseball footage used
with permission of Major League Baseball Properties, Inc.

Library of Congress Cataloging-in-Publication Data
Pastore, Frank, 1957-
  Shattered : struck down but not destroyed / Frank Pastore with Ellen
Vaughn.
     p. cm.
  Includes bibliographical references and index.
  ISBN 978-1-58997-611-5 (alk. paper)
  1. Pastore, Frank, 1957- 2. Christian biography—United States.
I. Vaughn, Ellen Santilli. II. Title.
  BR1725. P273
  [A3 2010]
  277.3'082092—dc22
  [B]
                                          2009051908

ISBN: 978-1-58997-611-5

Printed in the United States of America
4 5 6 7 8 9 / 15 14 13

To
Michael John Pastore,
my first grandson

★   ★   ★

The generational chains of sin and bondage
have been shattered.
I've written this book to inspire the hope
and vision of your generation,
and to remind you that our God is able
to do great and wonderful things.

CONTENTS

FOREWORD

Frank Pastore is the kind of leader we need most in today's Christian world—a clear thinker who talks straight. As a Major League™ baseball pitcher, Frank lived the American dream. He achieved the status symbols, prestige, and perks of the good life, as so many people today define it. But he was never satisfied . . . which led him on an insatiable quest for more. Then he began to realize he'd *never* have enough, and that his atheistic worldview was, in fact, pretty porous. He shoved that thought to the side.

Then came a career-ending injury, a disaster that led to a whole new way of thinking and living as a follower of Jesus Christ.

I can relate to Frank. I wasn't a player on the baseball diamond, of course. My journey to faith began when I sat in the office next to the president of the United States, having achieved my professional dreams, and I realized that my success was, in fact, rather hollow. It took the disaster of Watergate—a shattering, humbling experience—to lead me to the most fulfilling life I could have imagined, through the unlikely means of a prison sentence.

Usually, when God allows our dreams to be shattered, He has far better things in store for us, things we would not learn or achieve in any other way. You don't have to be a professional athlete or a special counsel to the president to know this. Everyone can relate to the pain of seeing a dream die. And hopefully, reading this book will help you see how God can use our greatest pains and defeats for our greatest gain, and that the life of the kingdom of God is lived in an entirely different dimension and on entirely different terms than life according to the values of this world.

I remember the first time I was a guest on Frank's radio show. I was expecting a routine Christianese interview, the type of thing I'd done a thousand times. I expected this ex-jock, prime-time host to be predictable. But I was struck immediately by the depth of Frank's questions and the scope of his understanding. This was no ordinary interview. This guy knew his stuff. He knew *my* stuff!

Since then we've become good friends and colleagues. Frank Pastore is not just a big-league player; he's a big-league thinker. He sees the larger picture and the context in which Christianity needs to be proclaimed and lived. Frank is a brother whose heart beats with the passion of my heart—worldview. He's asking the right questions; he gets the big issues. He has a fast mind and is well versed on current events and how they play out from a Christian perspective.

If there was ever a time when believers need this kind of discernment, it's now. America is caught in the perfect cultural storm. We have a financial meltdown caused largely by moral failures in government, on Wall Street, and in the public sector. We're paying the bill for decades of self-indulgence, fueled by rampant relativism, rejection of the Christian work ethic, and materialism. And there's an army of Islamic jihadists at the gate; their greatest dream is to destroy Israel and the Western world.

We need fresh voices like Frank's, voices that can reinvigorate the church with a sense of hope, deeper discipleship, and worldview teaching. His radio program is fittingly called "the intersection of faith and reason"—just what we need most in today's world.

This is the spirit of Frank's book. It's also a great read—fun, fast, and a real page-turner. That's because Ellen Vaughn helped put

Frank's story into words. Since Ellen and I have been writing colleagues for more than 20 years, I can attest that no one can tell a story better than Ellen.

Frank Pastore is one of the fresh new voices in today's Christian market. He's the kind of person the church desperately needs. We can all relate to his story. It's hilarious, poignant, insightful—and most important, it's not really all about Frank. It's about a God who loves us enough to seek us out, draw us to Himself, and restore and heal our lives for a greater purpose beyond ourselves.

—CHUCK COLSON
Washington, DC
October 8, 2009

WITH GRATITUDE

In writing a book that spans the first 50 years of your life, you have the opportunity to reflect upon those signal events that have altered the course of your life and to remember those special people whose fingerprints have marked your soul.

I have done my best to share everything in here as accurately and honestly as I can, so any errors and omissions in this book are solely my own.

To my coauthor Ellen Vaughn—thanks for guiding me so well through the process of sharing my life's story thus far. You're a gifted professional and a joy to work with! And thanks to Lee, Emily, Haley, and Walker and the kids for letting me steal Ellen away from her far more important duties as wife and mother to write this book. I couldn't have done it without her.

To Jim Steck—thanks for caring enough to push hard. Thirty-five years later, I still carry the momentum from those early shoves.

To Larry Arnn, Charles Kesler, Harry Jaffa, and the rest of the Claremont Institute—thanks for your trailblazing, your leadership, and your generosity.

To David Rosales—thanks for your faithful teaching of the Word of God, week in, week out, over these past 20 years. You're more than my pastor; you're my friend.

To Dr. G—thanks for allowing the Lord to use you to teach me how to put Humpty Dumpty back together again.

To my boss, Terry Fahy—thanks for the shot to do a daily, drive-time radio talk show. I strive every day to remind you that you made the right decision. And thanks to the great KKLA team at Salem Los Angeles: Chuck Tyler; Richard Kennedy; Bob Hastings; Terry Harris; Dave McBride; my technical producer and engineer, Ann Aragon; and assistant Nate Hanson.

To my biker buddies and their wives, Mark and Cindy Stapleton, Bruce and Teresa Erickson, Dave and Merle Pentz, and Sean and Linda McDougal—it's great to know you guys are always right behind me!

To our close friends for more years than I dare to remember: Roger and Diane Ingolia, Don and Kristi Kase, Eldon and Pam Lahr, Mike and Joanie Morrell, John and Kim Pomierski, Joe and Veronica Roggeman, and Walt and Marty Russell,—hey, isn't it your turn to buy dinner?

To Andrew and Judy Arena, and their kids, Andrew Jr., Richie, and Melody, thanks for adopting me into your beautiful family when I was going through those dark minor-league years in Tampa. I sure miss Mom's paella!

To not only my extended family but to my dear friends Johnny and Staci Pignotti and Don and Marina Gardner—thanks for teaching me what it means to be part of a big family. I love you guys.

To my mother-in-law, Ann Pignotti—thanks for all your love and support, and for being our "Nina."

To my daughter-in-law, Jessica Pastore—thanks for answering my son's prayers for a delightful and godly wife.

To my kids, Frankie and Christina—I'm so proud of you both, and I love you both so much! It's great to see how wonderful you are despite all my shortcomings. As we all know, we can thank only your mom for that.

To my truest friend, my most trusted confidante, my most honest and insightful counselor, my life partner, my darling Gina—thank you for the wonderful life you have built for us. You are the rock of our family and the ongoing joy of my life.

To my two dads, John Pignotti and Frank Pastore—I wish you both were still here. I'd give almost anything to play catch with you guys just one more time, or to share a steak and a bowl of spaghetti, or just to watch a ball game with you. I miss you every day.

And, finally, Lord, thank You that as the Master Craftsman, You take the shattered fragments of our lives and recast them into beautiful mosaics, through which Your light shines, evident to all.

1

★ ★ ★

OUT OF THE BLUE

It was a clear blue day in Dodger Stadium, perfect for baseball. And my life was perfect too.

At age 26, I'd been pitching for the Cincinnati Reds for five years. I had a beautiful wife, a young son, and a baby on the way, a decent fastball, and the cars, condos, and cash of the good life in the fast lane. My dreams had come true.

I was cruising to a 3-1 victory, with two outs in the eighth inning. I threw a 2-1 fastball on the outside of the plate, something I'd done a thousand times before.

It's odd how life can change forever in the blink of an eye.

My pitch was 91 miles per hour. As Dodger Steve Sax swung and connected, the ball's impact exerted roughly 8,000 pounds of force on the bat in a hundredth of a second. The violent collision compressed the ball, changed its direction, and packed it with kinetic energy. Rocketing through the air at about 132 miles per hour, the baseball covered the 60 feet 6 inches from home plate to the pitcher's mound in less than an eighth of a second. I didn't even have time to blink.

As the ball blurred toward my head, I instinctively threw up my right arm to protect my face. If I hadn't, the ball would have split my forehead, and it's unlikely I would be writing this book, since I'd be dead.

The ball exploded against my right elbow like a hammer hitting a glass bottle.

There was an eerie silence in the stadium. All eyes, including mine, turned to watch the replay on the big video screen in left field. People gasped as they watched—again and again—the destruction of my precious pitching arm.

For the crowd, it was like a NASCAR wreck, a type of gruesome entertainment. For me, it was a bad dream unfolding in slow motion. As I cradled my elbow in agony, I could push the bone fragments around like broken pieces of a cookie in a plastic bag.

But of course the game must go on. As Tommy Hume, the Red's relief pitcher, made his way in from the bull-pen, my mind was as jumbled as the jigsaw pieces of bone in my arm.

"God!" a voice inside me screamed. "Why would You let this happen?"

And that made me madder still. Prayer was for weaklings and losers. The fact that my pitching elbow and my dreams were both shattered had nothing to do with God. I didn't believe in God. I was raging at Someone who didn't exist.

2

★ ★ ★

THE GREAT ADVENTURE

It's a long way from that day in Dodger Stadium to today, and you may be thinking that the last thing you need right now is a tome full of fond sports memories from a pro athlete, now geezer, reliving his few glory days on the field.

Believe me, if that's all there was to my story, I wouldn't bother writing it.

But this story was worth writing—and hopefully you'll find it worth reading—because it's really about what happens to all of us at some point. Pitching arms get randomly whacked. Careers end. Accidents, illness, and death destroy lives. Loved ones betray us. Relationships rupture. Kids break our hearts. We mess up. Life can be so hard, and sometimes the difference between what we want and what we get almost kills us.

So this is a story about brokenness and how sometimes the things you fear most can actually change your life for good. That's what happened with me—not just with the shattered elbow that eventually ended my pro sports career, but also in all kinds of ways over the years. Each shattering broke me apart . . . and then God put the pieces back together again, better and stronger than before.

I wish He would do His work in some other less painful way. I wish life were easy.

But it's not. Anybody who cheerfully tells you that you just "receive Jesus" and things will go smoothly and prosperously is either lying or has never read the Bible.

Don't get me wrong. I wouldn't trade my worst day as a Christian for my best day as a pagan. I've found the Christian life to be the greatest adventure I could ever have imagined, a journey so full of passion, power, and just plain fun that I cannot fathom why anyone would choose to believe anything else.

That leads to the second reason I wrote this book. I travel and speak a lot at conferences; I receive tons of e-mails in response to my daily radio show. A lot of people, particularly men, share their experiences with me, which has led me to believe that many Christians never get the big picture about their faith. They are satisfied with far too little. They think of Christianity as something like this: Jesus died for my sins, I received Him, I'm going to heaven when I die, and till then, I'm supposed to sin less.

Well, I'm all for sinning less, believe me. But the purely personal lens of faith misses so much! It reduces the great drama of the gospel down to me, me, and me: It's all about *my* salvation, *my* sanctification. It's Christianity for narcissists.

The gospel of Jesus Christ is about the ultimate victory of real, robust good over sick, twisted evil. It's about justice for those who can't speak for themselves; it's about peace with God and peace in relationships with other human beings. It's about right racial relationships and the care of God's green earth. It speaks to economics, philosophy, government, and law. The big gospel vision informs everything from our birth through our dying breath; it encompasses eternal dimensions we can't yet perceive.

The Big Story is not about what leads the daily newscast or gets the buzz on talk radio. The real story is the cosmic battle between good and evil—a conflict in which *we* are invited to participate.

The gospel is a lot bigger than fire insurance—you know, making sure we get to go to heaven when we die. It's a lot more than just getting saved, great as that is. Sometimes, as I said, we're satisfied with far too little. We need a bigger perspective of what the kingdom of God is all about. Let me give you an illustration.

A long time ago, when our son, Frankie, was three and I was pitching for the Reds, I had an off day during spring training in Florida. I took Frankie to Disney World. I had talked it up for days, telling him about Mickey and Minnie and the monorail and all the cool rides and Disney characters. He was pumped. I strapped him into his car seat and drove toward Orlando, getting more and more excited every minute.

"Are we there yet?" he kept asking.

"Not yet," I'd say. "Almost."

We finally rolled into the big parking lot. I pulled Frankie out of his car seat and carried him to the tram that took us to the gate. We bought the tickets, got our hands stamped, and pushed through the turnstiles. We'd finally made it to Disney World.

If you've been there, you can visualize it. As you pass through the turnstiles, there's a large patio area with two tunnels, one on either side, leading into the park. There are beautiful plantings and bright flowers, and if you're lucky, some of the Disney characters are entertaining the crowd.

Frankie's eyes were huge. He looked up and saw the big Mickey Mouse face made out of flowers on the hill. Just then, the Disney World train pulled into the station just above Mickey's face. The engine spouted plumes of white-cotton smoke into the azure sky. The whistle blew.

Frankie loved trains. He was so overwhelmed by it all that he was on overload, like a T1 data line plugged into a 286 computer chip.

I grabbed his hand, thrilled about what the day had in store for us.

"Come on, buddy," I said. "Let's go!"

He didn't move. My normally compliant son locked his little legs and stood there in rigid defiance. Tears squirted out of his eyes.

"No," he said, slowly shaking his head from side to side.

I knelt down and grabbed his shoulders. "Frankie, listen," I said. "This is just the *beginning* of Disney World. There's tons of cool stuff inside. C'mon, buddy!"

He didn't get it. As far as he was concerned, we'd come all this way to arrive at this special place. It couldn't get any better than this, and here was Dad, ready to leave. He was gonna stand his ground.

I understood. But since I outweighed him by 200 pounds, I picked him up and started through the tunnel that would take us to Main Street.

"I don't wanna go!" he screamed. "No! No! No!"

People were staring. Frankie was crying and beating his fists on my back, the most miserable little person in the "happiest place on earth!"

It was the longest 20 seconds of my life, but as we emerged from the tunnel, there was Cinderella's castle, its towers white against the blue sky. There was Goofy walking right up Main Street in his giant shoes. There was the Matterhorn roller coaster in the distance, with people screaming in joy as they rode the bobsleds. There was candy, hot dogs, music, dancing, bright colors everywhere—more than we could possibly take in.

Frankie's mouth was wide open. "Ooohhh!" he finally managed. "Come on in, buddy!" I yelled.

And for the rest of the day, I took my son from wonder to wonder. Around every turn was a new adventure. Each ride we got on, each food we tasted, each character we met, Frankie would smile so big I thought he'd burst.

Despite all the sugar he ate that day, the little guy crashed right after sundown. He fell asleep on my shoulder, exhausted, a smile still on his face.

I've heard from a lot of Christians who think the whole point of Christianity is just to get saved, to get "in." They're like my son at the entry area of Disney World. They don't know there are adventures beyond the entrance.

And like my showing Frankie around Disney World, exploring new thrills at every turn, God wants to take us farther up and farther in to the adventures in His kingdom. Our experience won't be perfect until the ultimate restoration, when sin and death are banished forever. But life with the King in His kingdom begins right *now!*

When I was an atheist, I knew nothing of this adventure. I thought Christians were stupid and Christianity was a bunch of man-made rules. But when I learned the truth, what pulled me in was the big picture of it all.

This is a team I want to play for, I thought. *This is worth fighting for.*

This is worth dying for. Magnificent. Awesome. This is what I've been looking for my whole life. I've got to be part of it.

My story begins about as far from magnificent and awesome as you can get. It begins under the less-than-tender care and tutelage of a sociopath who would have ruined me for life had God not intervened.

3

★ ★ ★

FAT KIDS CAN DREAM TOO

When I was growing up, truth was a stranger to me. Conceived out of wedlock by a devious manipulator who'd been married four or five times, I was raised with so many lies that I had no idea what was true and what wasn't.

My mom told me she liked my dad because of his money. He liked her physical assets. Because of this grand love, they married, and I was majestically conceived on their wedding night.

The reality was that she hooked up with my dad, a high school dropout, after her fourth failed marriage. She had been struggling to make it as a single mom with a young daughter in Los Angeles in the mid-1950s and "accidentally" got pregnant with me. She considered having another abortion but got married instead. The rest was a miserable tangle of lies, deceit, and rootless transitions throughout Southern California.

For all practical purposes, I was an only child; I did have one half-sister from one of my mom's previous marriages. She moved out when I was 3 and she was 15. So I was a latchkey kid from the time I was four. I'd walk home from preschool and sit on the porch. From there I could see the kids coming home from school, and I'd yell out to them, "Hey! Come over and play with me!"

They never did.

So I'd play with Elrod, my imaginary friend. He was always there for me. Elrod and I would build models and race my Matchbox cars. Elrod raced with my left hand, and I raced with my right. I usually won because my right arm was stronger.

When Elrod and I got hungry, we'd go in the kitchen and have a big bag of Cheez Doodles and a box of Cracker Jack popcorn, digging deep for the prize inside. I'd have Ding Dongs and ice cream for breakfast, frozen dinners or the Sizzler big-kid platter for dinner. I was told there were starving children in Africa, so I obediently cleaned my plate, drank a quart of milk, and put away two pieces of pie.

I never did make the connection between stuffing my face and helping hungry children, but my mom always gave me supersized praise for chowing down. I became an overachiever at overeating. So it was pretty sad that I didn't learn about brushing my teeth until I was in third grade. My mother had never thought to mention it.

When I finally went to the dentist for the first time, I had 21 cavities and a serious buildup of doughnut-inspired plaque. My mother's idea of hygiene was standing at the kitchen sink, smoking a Tareyton with a half-inch ash, and sponging herself a little before she went to work in the morning. She reeked.

When she got home, she ranted about her boss, men in general, my dad in particular, and how unfair life was. She'd escape the injustice of it all by withdrawing into her world of books. She was always reading, in the big chair in the living room or in her nest in her bedroom, wearing a huge muumuu and smoking one cigarette after another until there was a pile of ash around her like Mount Vesuvius.

The first time that I realized my mother's version of reality was seriously warped was when I was in the fifth grade. I had signed up to sing a solo in the school talent show. I knew I would shine; after all, my mom had told me that I could do anything. She praised me a lot, in direct proportion to the scorn she heaped on my dad. She had taught me to believe that if things didn't go well for me, it was always somebody else's fault.

So, in my 10-year-old brain, I conceived of myself as a great singer. I was set to wow the tryout judges with my audition of the hit ballad of the day, "Born Free."

I arrived in the tryout room. As I waited my turn to get up on the stage, I dimly began to wonder just what I was doing there. I'd never sung anything before in front of other people. I didn't even know if I *could* sing.

It was my turn. The judges, mostly nice older women, smiled encouragingly at me. The lady at the piano nodded and launched into the opening bars of the song.

Dry-mouthed, I missed my cue. She started over. I missed it again. What she was playing didn't sound anything like the song on the radio. I guess I was waiting for the orchestral lead-in that never came.

On the third try, I somehow got it going.

"BORN FREE!" I warbled. "AS FREE AS THE GRASS GROWS! AS FREE AS THE WIND BLOWS! BORN FREE, TO FOL-LOW YOUR H-E-A-A-A-RT!"

As I screeched that last note, paint peeling off the walls of the room, I saw the judges' faces. All the nice ladies, who would have accepted just about anything, were in absolute shock, their eyebrows up and their mouths frozen open in little Os, like squirrels who've been hit by tractor trailers.

I realized that I wasn't just bad; I was terrible, worthy of pity. The nice ladies' eyes said it all: "How could this poor child ever believe that he could sing? What mother would allow her child to embarrass himself like this? Who could be so cruel?"

I could *not* sing. My mom had lied to me.

If I'd been older, maybe it would have been funny. But I was 10—a really young, sheltered, mama's boy 10.

My eyes welled with tears. I ran off the stage, toward home. Where else could I go? But in that moment of terrible truth, I felt lost. I didn't know who I really was, what I really could do . . . If my mom could be this wrong about my singing, what else was she wrong about? What else had she lied about?

I had always believed everything she told me, but now I realized, as much as a fifth grader can, that I had a big problem. I couldn't trust my mother's version of life. It was as if I'd always looked in the mirror and seen myself a certain way, as well as the landscape all around me—and now that familiar picture was shattered.

But life went on.

Thanks to my rigorous high-doughnut diet, I was seriously chubby by the time I entered junior high. Every morning I rubbed Vitalis in my hair and carefully combed it so I'd look like my TV idol Robert Wagner. Then I'd put on the clothes my mom bragged to me that she stole regularly from the men's department of the Bond's clothing store where she worked. These were like powder-blue cardigans, polyester turtlenecks, and cuffed plaid trousers. Oversized wingtips with limp brown socks.

This was in Southern California in the '60s. All the other kids wore jeans, Hang Ten shirts, and flip-flops. I looked like a refugee from the American Association of Geeky Middle-aged Men.

In the midst of this nerdy nightmare, I did have one thing going for me: I could throw stuff really hard. Even though I was doughy, I was a lethal combatant in our war games in the lemon groves near our house. I was the slow heavy artillery, lobbing long-distance lemon bombs with amazing accuracy at the quicker kids on the front lines. At any moment, if I wanted, I could absolutely nail any of the enemy kids who tormented me.

Later, in Little League, I could drill kids right where I wanted, in the thigh if I was just slightly mad, or in the ribs if I was really ticked. I dreamed of playing baseball in the Major Leagues.™ After school, while I was waiting for my dad to come home from his ironworker job, I'd throw a million pitches against the block wall in our yard, pretending I was Tom Seaver pitching to Johnny Bench.

My mother told me those dreams were stupid. She wanted me to go to college and make something of myself so I wouldn't become a loser like my dad.

I never did really see what was so bad about my dad. And I somehow knew that having big dreams wasn't stupid. I just had no idea how to achieve them.

4

★ ★ ★

LIFE IN THE WITNESS PROTECTION PROGRAM

My dad had left high school during the Depression to help his family in LA's Italian ghetto. By others' accounts he was a generous guy with a big laugh and a great smile. But as far as my mom was concerned, there was nothing remotely good about him. She called him "the peasant" and taught me, through relentless repetition, that he was a worthless loser. I wasn't sure about that, since my dad was my Little League coach and he actually spent time playing catch with me. We never talked about anything significant, but at least we had a baseball connection. It was only after his death—once I had shaken off my mom's malignant thinking—that I mourned what our relationship could have been.

Both my grandfathers had died before I was born, and both grandmothers had died by the time I was 10. My dad had a younger brother and sister, but I rarely saw them. Let's just say that my mom had no focus on the family—not ours, my dad's, or her own. She was one of 12 siblings. I met most of them for the first time when I was 11 and she drove me back to her home in Birmingham, Alabama, because someone had died and she actually decided to attend the funeral.

Mom had run away from home at age 17 to marry the town gambler. My grandfather had annulled it, and then when my mother turned 18, she left for good. She didn't graduate from high school. As for religion, she was raised Southern Baptist, but exchanged her faith for a cynical, outspoken atheism.

That's about all I know of her history.

Anyway, here I was at this funeral, 11 years old and needing an org chart to know who was who. There were dozens of aunts, uncles, and cousins. It was so alien, like those big families you see on TV. They knew each other, loved each other, and cared about each other.

I felt—and looked—as if I were from another planet. Mom had gotten me three sets of matching shorts and shirts in pastel blue, green, and yellow. Striped. I looked like a chubby Easter egg, or Charlie Brown on steroids. I remember her telling me several times during the trip, "I want them to know we have money."

So, growing up, I didn't have "family" in the true sense of the word. Nor did we have any family friends. I don't remember a single time anyone came to the house to visit Mom, or her chatting on the phone with someone. I don't think she had a true friend in her life.

No surprise, then, that my parents didn't do things with other couples. If my dad had anyone over, or if any of his buddies stopped by the house spontaneously, he caught my mom's wrath about it later. My mother didn't like me having friends over to play, either.

One evening my mother decided we needed new carpeting. She told me to put the stopper in the tub and turn on the faucet, full force. Meanwhile, she waited in the driveway, the motor running in the Riviera.

"Where are we going?" I asked. "What about the water?"

"Get in," she said coldly.

I obeyed.

We went out for an all-you-can-eat buffet, came home, and sure enough, the house was flooded. My mom worked the insurance company, and presto! New carpeting.

As you can imagine, we moved every time my mom's lies caught up with her. By the time I entered high school, I had lived in 12 houses. As the perennial new kid in school, I found that my geeky look didn't exactly help me fit in.

But my mother called the shots. She'd come home from work or somewhere and announce to my dad and me that we were moving. We'd moan, but then we'd do what she wanted. I don't know why my dad was so compliant or why he took all the verbal abuse she threw at him.

Life in my family was like growing up in the Witness Protection Program: Never let anyone get too close. Don't reveal too much about yourself. Don't contact your extended family. Don't allow visitors. Don't make any friends; keep them just as acquaintances.

It's odd—here I am today, basically a gregarious extrovert who loves being around people. I was the same person back then, in a kid body with a kid's perspective. I didn't know that things could be different. I didn't know that my experience of life and relationships was warped. I trusted my mother.

After all, she was my mom. Even though she was big, mad, and foul, she was the only reality I knew, and she and my dad, strange as they were, were my only experience of what it meant to be part of a family.

5

★ ★ ★

NO CRYING IN BASEBALL

My dad was born in 1914 and played semipro baseball in the '30s and '40s before breaking a rib in a barroom fight the night before his professional tryout, which ended his baseball career. So he went back to his first career as an ironworker. Before he met my mom, he was the foreman for building jobs all over California, as well as Saudi Arabia, Morocco, and the Middle East.

He was also a star with Union Local no. 433 in Los Angeles. Back then the unions played against each other on the ball field, and so my dad had a solid job, hit the ball on the weekends, and made a pretty good bachelor's life for himself . . . until he got tangled up in my mother's troubled web.

He was 43 when I was born, so when I was a little boy, people always thought he was my grandpa. I remember when I was about 7, we were playing catch one day, and the ball went over the long, high concrete wall between our house and the neighbors' yard. I was fat and hated heights; I couldn't climb a wall if you paid me. So Dad just hopped the wall. Effortlessly. Then, coming back, he walked down the narrow wall for about 50 feet, as fast as I could run down a sidewalk. If he could walk the high steel 15 stories off the ground, I guess a 6-foot block wall was no big deal. I stared up at him; at that moment he was like Superman to me. He was 50 years old.

We played catch just about every day. I'd wait outside for him to come home from work, throwing my ball against the wall and dreaming of pitching to Johnny Bench. I could always hear Dad coming. He drove only Buick Rivieras once they came out in 1963, and he always installed custom dual-exhaust glass packs so they sounded like muscle-car hot rods. He kept them spotless.

Dad would be in his work clothes, a khaki-colored Dickies set with matching shirt and pants; rolled-up sleeves, work boots with leather laces only to the ankle, Ray-Bans, a half-smoked King Edward Imperial in his mouth, and a big smile, with bright white teeth.

He'd get out of the car and stroll over to greet me. We'd toss the ball around for a while, with him on one knee. Then we'd chamois off his car and mess around in the garage. If it was baseball season, we'd spend the afternoon and evening listening to Vin Scully and the Dodgers.

Dad was always my baseball coach growing up. It started with the Beavers in West Covina the summer I turned 9 in 1966. I still have the team picture, right alongside my Major League™ shots from the '80s.

Every Saturday we'd go to Orange Julius after the game, and the big thing for me was to order a raw egg in my juice. Other kids my age thought that was totally gross, but I thought it was cool because my dad did it. The raw egg didn't help me much. My earliest baseball-game memory comes from the summer I turned 10. I was playing for the Tigers. The game was on the line, last inning, and we were down by one. I was up to bat, there were two outs, and the bases were loaded. My palms were sweaty, the crowd was roaring as if it were the last game of the World Series . . . and I struck out. Again.

The truth was, I was scared of the ball. I flinched and stepped in the bucket on every pitch. A total wuss. So there I was, sitting on the bench, head down, eyes full of tears. I didn't go out onto the field with my coach and the rest of my teammates to shake hands with the other players. I just sat on the bench, sulking and crying, my jacket pulled up over my head, like a turtle hiding in its shell.

A shadow appeared in front of me. My dad ripped the jacket off my head and pulled my chin up with his ham-sized hand.

"Get your head up," he said. "There's no crying in baseball."

With that he yanked me up to my feet and marched me out toward our car. Tears still ran down my face, other kids were making fun of me for being a crybaby, and as we got closer to the parking lot, I ran as fast as I could to escape it all. I vowed to never, ever embarrass myself on the baseball field again.

And I didn't . . . for many, many years at least.

By the next year, I was really good. I made the all-star team as an 11-year-old. At 12, I threw five no-hitters, two of them perfect games. But we lost our first all-star game that year, thanks to a great pitcher who threw a no-hitter against us.

It didn't seem fair—this guy was a giant on the field, and he was already shaving, and we were little peach-fuzz boys. (I still remember him, though, because we ended up going to the same high school and becoming friends. His name was Steve Schiro. He left baseball and went into business to help his friend Bill Gates start a little company called Microsoft.)

Well, by age 13, I wasn't yet a manly man like Steve, but I'd started to grow a little. I was about five foot nine, and one day I needed to warm up at the start of an inning, but the catcher wasn't ready. So Dad came out to catch while I pitched . . . something he had done my whole life.

Dad smiled, his cigar clamped between his white teeth, and kneeled down on one knee. I threw a few pitches, each one successively harder.

"Okay, Frankie," he shouted. "Let 'er loose!"

I threw the ball as hard as I could. Dad caught it in the palm of the catcher's mitt. It was a perfect strike. He collapsed to the ground, pulling the glove off his left hand and cradling his wrist with his right. I had popped some blood vessels in his hand and hyperextended his thumb; it was already turning purple.

The coaches helped Dad get up and get some ice on his hand. As he did, he threw a big grin my way.

"D—!" he yelled. "This hurts like h—, but *I am so proud of you!*"

He never caught me again.

It was a huge coming-of-age moment. But most of my early adolescent years were not as memorable. They were an ongoing geeky nightmare, like one of those dreams you desperately want to awake from, but in my case I couldn't, because it was my life.

My mother tended to uproot me at just about the worst possible time . . . So there I was, fall of seventh grade. School had already started, and I was the new kid. Again. But junior high is so much more vicious than elementary school. It's sort of like life in Sparta— merciless, with the weak winnowed out and fed to the strong for breakfast.

Once the guys at my new school realized that I wasn't a fighter, and I wasn't good at football or basketball because I couldn't run, I was doomed. Sometimes nonathletes were accepted if they were really cute, a Bobby Sherman type that the girls liked, or witty, sort of like a court jester for the popular kids. I was neither, just a pudgy kid wandering around in matching shorts sets or plaid trousers and wingtips, thanks to Mom.

I was the last kid picked for teams in PE. The cool kids made constant fun of me. It's surprising I survived until January, when Little League tryouts began. All the new kids in the league had to go. But, as with so many things in my childhood, my mom had come up with a scheme to game the system. She got my dad to ask around and find out who the best team was; we needed a good catcher who could "hold" my fastball—meaning I didn't throw so hard that he couldn't catch me—and one other good pitcher. I already knew back then that good pitching beats good hitting.

Dad did the research. He took me to an elementary school to pitch for the manager, Mr. Van Duin. Dad made sure no other kids from the league were around. We didn't want word getting out that I was any good. Mr. Van Duin's son Ted was the other good pitcher. He came, and I remember the "wow" in his eyes when I cut loose the heat.

On the day of the official tryouts, all the managers, coaches, and parents were watching to grade the kids for the draft. Dad had told me to blow the audition. So, three ground balls, three muffs. Later, three dropped fly balls, and three bad swings and misses. I may have even batted left-handed—I can't remember—but it would have fit the pattern. I didn't pitch at all since I couldn't fake being bad at that.

All this killed me inside. I was faking who I really was, and I hated it. No one thought I was any good, which didn't give me the payoff I was looking forward to at school. But when the draft came, Mr. Van Duin easily picked me up in the first round, with chuckles around the room, I'm told, from the other managers, who thought he'd made a terrible mistake.

My dad and Mr. Van Duin were the coach and the manager for the team. We took the championship. Ted and I were the best pitchers in the league, and I led the league in homers. I was the ace of the league, and with a bunch of write-ups in the paper, I finally got the respect I had sought.

We were a baseball family. In spite of our crazy dysfunction, we probably looked perfectly normal to outsiders: the smiling mom, the proud dad, the son who was a pretty decent pitcher. At home, though, the scenes weren't always so wholesome. I remember working with my dad in the garage one night and getting on his nerves. He was pretty patient with me, but I kept bugging him about something, trying to get under his skin.

I succeeded. He yelled at me to "cut it out!" and pushed my shoulder just as my mom came into the garage to get something. I was a pretty good manipulator—she had trained me well. I staggered after my dad pushed me, and then I fell down, whimpering a little.

My mom grabbed a bat and came at my dad. "You get your hands off him!" she said slowly and deliberately, full of cold, controlled rage. My mom never yelled, which somehow made her fury more terrifying. "If you ever touch him again," she told my dad, "I'll break your legs while you're asleep!"

So our home life wasn't exactly healthy. But our baseball life was all-American, apple pie. We were at the ballpark together every night during the season.

Upland, California, was like most small towns. There was a good part and a bad part. In Upland, the dividing line was Foothill Boulevard. If you lived north of Foothill, you had money; if you lived south of Foothill, you didn't.

I lived *way* south of Foothill, and played for the Upland American

League. It wasn't quite the wrong side of the tracks, but I felt the stigma. If you lived north of Foothill, you played in Foothill Little League, our rivals. I wondered just how good these kids really were who lived in the "good" part of town.

When we played them in the big all-star game, I found out. They were tough, and we lost in a close game. One good thing came out of that contest, though. I earned the respect of the Foothill players: I was the toughest pitcher they'd ever faced.

The following season, my goal was to lead all the pitching categories. I had found out something new about myself: I didn't just love baseball. I didn't just love to pitch. I loved to *win*, and I would push myself, pull myself, beat my brains out, work as hard as I could and harder, do whatever it took to be the best. I vowed to do everything in my power to become the pitcher I wanted to be.

What I didn't yet know about life was how things outside of your control can take you down. I was about to find out, though, from the vantage point of a concrete bathroom floor, watching my own blood run, in a thin little river, down the dirty drain.

6

★ ★ ★

GETTING JUMPED, PART ONE

It wasn't exactly a Mob hit, but it was still a pretty grim experience for a 13-year-old.

It was April 1971, the Saturday after our weeklong Easter break—which was still called "Easter" vacation back then, not "spring break." Not that it mattered to me; I was an atheist, as was any decent, halfway intelligent, self-respecting person, according to my mother.

Anyway, on that Saturday, I'd had an especially great game, and we had beat the pants off a big, strong Hispanic team called Antimite, except back then we just called them the Chicano team.

My teammates had been backslapping each other; we were pretty wound up. I had to go to the bathroom, so I walked into the little eight-by-eight-foot bathroom at the back of the snack bar by myself, not thinking much about anything except how well I'd pitched and how happy I was that we'd won.

I walked toward the urinals. I heard the sound of the lock being turned in the bathroom door. Four huge Chicano guys grabbed me; two of them held me down while the other two hit me over and over and over.

They smacked me only a few times in the face. My right eye got swollen shut, and blood ran down my neck from a cut on my lip . . . but mostly they focused on my right arm. My pitching arm. They pummeled me as hard as they could, going after the arm, the shoulder, the biceps, grunting and cussing at me in Spanish. It sounded like somebody swinging a hammer and hitting raw meat, 40, 50 times.

It took forever, but at the same time it was fast. They jumped up, unlocked the door, and ran away.

It wasn't hard to identify them; they'd been wearing their black-and-white Antimite jackets, and so it was pretty clear they were from the team we'd just beaten. I even recognized one of them from school.

My parents were out of their minds with rage. My arm turned black and blue, as if someone had smeared ink all over my shoulder and biceps. I couldn't comb my hair or brush my teeth, let alone pitch. My season was over. The thugs' mission was accomplished, and their message was clear.

I had never been in a fight before. I didn't even know how to punch. But after Easter vacation, I had my eye out for that Antimite kid who went to my school. We weren't in any of the same classes, and he was always with his Chicano buddies. In the early '70s in that area, there were a lot of brown-white racial tensions in the schools. There were lots of fights, even full-blown riots with dozens of students facing off and going out of control. We all knew whose turf was whose, where to walk, which bathrooms were brown and which were white.

So I never got close to my attacker until the beginning of eighth grade. I had grown four inches over the summer, and there he was, like a gift, sitting in my new first-period class. He had been eyeing me and snickering since the jumping, but now without his buddies around him, he wasn't so tough.

The next day, before the teacher came in, I walked over to the kid's desk. The whole class was watching.

"I know it was you," I said, leaning over him while he sat in his chair. I drew back and gave him the hardest closed-fist punch to the left cheek that I could. It knocked him out of the chair and onto the floor. I was on him in a second . . . and then the teacher walked in.

We both got sent to the principal's office, but of course he got off because eyewitnesses said I was the aggressor. Which I was. I got suspended for four weeks—much longer than a normal sentence in a case like this.

The principal was afraid the whole thing would ignite another round of race fights on campus. He obviously didn't know how unpopular I was with the white kids . . . No one would have been interested in fighting for me, of all people.

The principal called my mother, who swept into his office like a large avenging angel. I told him the whole backstory, and she backed me up. He got it. He declared me suspended but said I could serve my suspension in the teachers' conference room. I could spend the whole school day there and keep up with my classwork. Later he told me that was the best way he could protect me; he was worried the bad guys would kill me.

Mom picked me up every day after school. We all knew that if I was ever caught unprotected, like walking or riding my bike, the Chicanos would beat the tar out of me or knife me.

As eighth grade ended, I remember the glaring eyes, the whispers, the feeling of always having to look over my shoulder. The Chicanos egged my house just so I'd know that they knew where I lived. They got the message to me: "You may have been able to hide in junior high, but we're gonna get you at Upland." I realized that once I got to Upland High School, they would either mess up my pitching arm for life, not just a season, or they'd actually kill me.

I wasn't too excited about either of those options.

My mom had chosen to keep my dad in the dark about most of this, claiming that he'd beat somebody up and make the whole thing even worse than it was. And as messed up as I thought my mom was psychologically, she was entirely "normal" in the sense that she didn't want her only son killed, maimed, or dismembered limb by limb.

That was a relief.

So my mom decided I should go to Damien High School, which ended up being one of the key shaping factors in my life.

It's pretty ironic now when I look back and see that God propelled me to Damien by means of blunt force—as in the Chicano gang. But of course back then, I didn't believe in God and wouldn't have had a clue about how He works in people's lives. Nor would I have cared. But He got me where He wanted me, through some pretty creative—and painful—means.

Damien was the private Catholic boys' high school in our area, home to great sports and excellent academics. Some of the best baseball players my age were going there. These were the kids I admired. Steve Schiro, the hairy man-teen, awesome pitcher, with unborn dreams of Microsoft dancing in his brain. Danny Monroe, a great hitter, who would later graduate from Notre Dame, make a fortune in banking in New York, and retire at age 40. And, of course, Johnny Pignotti.

Johnny was an amazing baseball player, a great hitter, and the best catcher in our area. He was also smart, cool, good-looking, funny, popular, and a girl magnet. Everything I was not. But there was something about Johnny that drew me, rather than intimidated me. I wanted to be like him. He had everything I wanted, including his family . . . and his little sister, Gina.

But I'm getting a bit ahead of my story.

7

★ ★ ★

BECOMING A CATHOLIC ATHEIST

Damien High School presented a few obstacles. First, it was expensive. We didn't have much money, but my parents were proud of me having the opportunity to go there; they said we'd just sacrifice to make it work.

But the second and biggest obstacle was that we weren't Catholic. We weren't anything. My mother had been raised as a nice Southern Baptist girl in Birmingham, Alabama, but something had gone seriously wrong somewhere along her spiritual journey. As I've said, she was outspoken about her disdain for religious faith. It was stupid, for wimps and weaklings. Mom had taught me that evolution and chance were the only explanations for life, which was basically painful and pointless. From her perspective, the only goals, really, were to accumulate as much stuff as you could and have as many pleasures along the way as you could afford. In the end, when you died, you just ceased to exist. Nothing.

And in spite of being from a typical Catholic immigrant family, my dad didn't have any religious inclinations, except in his cussing. He didn't go to church either. Ever. We had never gone to any kind of services as a family. We didn't own a Bible. We never prayed over meals, sicknesses, or even ball games.

In spite of the fact that God didn't exist, however, I see now that He was in the game.

We moved to a new house north of Foothill Boulevard, on the better side of Upland. I took the entrance exam to get into Damien, passed, and was admitted. We were told that tuition would be a couple hundred bucks a month cheaper if we were Catholic.

It was time to get religion.

Mom told me to follow her lead. We met with the priests at Damien every week, proclaiming our newfound love for faith. We lied baldly about every aspect of the catechism. I watched my mom effortlessly say she believed in things I knew she didn't, only to laugh about it with me afterward, proud of being such a smooth liar. We passed whatever tests they gave us, and then somehow, at the end of it all, we were Catholic.

When my heroes Johnny Pignotti, Danny Monroe, and Steve Schiro found out that I was joining them at Damien, they told me I had to try out for the freshman football team. It was the first thing they had ever asked me to join them in, so I quickly agreed. I had played flag football once or twice. I couldn't run, but I was sort of big for my age, and I figured I might get in better physical condition. Besides, how hard could it be?

Football practice started with "Hell Week."

Johnny told me they'd pick me up at seven o'clock in the morning. He said that since there'd be lots of conditioning, I should eat a big breakfast with lots of eggs, pancakes, and milk. I obediently woke up early, which didn't come naturally, and stuffed myself. I was ready to go when Steve's older brother picked us up in his old Ford Falcon with the really cool four-track tape deck blasting Crosby, Stills, Nash, and Young.

It didn't take long for me to make my mark. On the second lap around the football field, after doing all kinds of push-ups, sit-ups, and assorted contortions, I grandly tossed my enormous breakfast in all its half-digested glory. I was the first one to throw up. Actually, I was the only one to throw up. Eighty guys were there. It was the first day of high school for athletes. So much for making a good first impression.

Steve and Johnny laughed so hard, they almost threw up too. Eating a big breakfast is exactly what *not* to do, and I'd been stupid enough to fall for it. I was a dream come true for them, not only because of my flamboyant regurgitation, but because I was like a giant marshmallow: slow, fat, puffy, and white. Plus, I knew nothing about football. These guys had played against each other since they were toddlers, and I was like a large, slow life-form from another planet.

I wanted to quit within about five minutes of arriving that first morning. The coaches and kids all egged me on: "Hey, Pastore, why don't you just quit and go home and do something you're good at, like watching TV!"

But somewhere inside my body of dough was a core of steel. There was no way I was going to quit. I had never been more sore, even when the Chicano guys beat me up. I had never been as tired as I was that first night after practice. I crawled toward my bed like a giant slug, leaving a slimy trail of sweat behind me.

But a miracle began to occur. Over the next two weeks of conditioning, I lost a ton of baby fat. I started to get in shape for the first time in my life. A bunch of kids quit, and I had some status simply by being a survivor. Maybe there was hope.

No, there wasn't.

The coaches broke out the pads, and we started to tackle and hit. I hated it, and even though I wasn't quite the marshmallow I used to be, it was pretty clear that football was just not my thing.

The last straw came when I had to go up against this big, strong guy on what they called the "board drill." Two guys would straddle a long plank on the ground, get in their stance facing each other, and the idea was to push the other guy back across the end of the board with everything he had.

The coach called me out of the group to go up against this monster, who would become our starting defensive nose tackle, Frank Flores. The whistle blew, there was this huge crash, and everything went black. I woke up staring at the beautiful blue California sky, dreaming a little.

Flores had hit me so hard that I had done a beautiful backward somersault and landed on the back of my neck. If God had existed back then, it would have been a miracle that I was able to walk.

The next morning my left shoulder was black and blue, about the same colors the Chicano gang had rendered my right arm when they beat me up. My parents were *not* pleased. They had grudgingly allowed me to play football just as a means to get in shape. They lived in fear of me hurting my pitching arm and ending my baseball career. They could see that if Flores had hit me on the right shoulder rather than the left, I probably wouldn't have ever been able to pitch again.

I quit before ever playing a single down in full formation. For the record, I was the eighth string right tackle. I have a photo with my shaved head to prove it.

Freshman year was tough. I didn't make many new friends at my new school, and even though Steve and Johnny tolerated me and respected my baseball ability, I wasn't really part of their group. They were the cool, popular guys in the honors courses, the class officers. I was a nobody. A nobody with acne. Giant cystic acne. The people who did talk to me called me "pizza face" behind my back.

In the fall of my freshman year, Damien High invited two Catholic girls' schools to a dance. I had been dancing with a cute girl for a few fast songs, hoping to get the chance for a slow dance. I'd been flailing away to "Jumpin' Jack Flash" and had worked up a pretty good sweat. I was wearing one of my dad's white long-sleeved silk shirts and had used some of my mom's CoverGirl face makeup to paint over my acne.

The fast song ended, and the slow-dance classic of that era, "Color My World," started. Sweat dripping, I wiped my face with both sleeves and grabbed the cute girl. We slow danced, and it was wonderful. The song ended.

Just as I was tilting my head down to try to kiss the girl, the lights came back on. Her eyes popped as wide as dinner plates, her head flew back in revulsion, and her mouth dropped. There was no way she was going to kiss me. She began backing away, staring at my arms.

I looked down, and there on both sleeves, on this beautiful white shirt, were smears of what looked like moist brown paint. She gasped and kept backing away. Everyone around us turned to look. The circle around us grew larger and larger, the gasps turned to giggles, then laughter, then outright howling. It was like being surrounded by hyenas.

There I was, CoverGirl liquid makeup smeared all over both arms of my shirt, sort of like the impression of Jesus' face on Saint Veronica's towel, except entirely different. I fled to the bathroom, cowering in a stall, and then the bathroom was full of taunting guys going nuts.

It was far worse than getting jumped by the Chicanos. This was emotional agony. That night ended, eventually, but then on Monday morning, everyone in the entire school knew about me wearing makeup to the fall dance. I was the absolute laughingstock of the campus.

Now, of course, I can laugh about the Great CoverGirl Dance Incident and other silly stories. But the pain I remember from those times of adolescent rejection still cuts like a razor.

I somehow survived the fall, and baseball season rolled around. I had grown from five feet nine inches to about six feet. I'd been working out with weights at home and had lost the marshmallow look. I couldn't wait for our game against the Antimite team, whose members had jumped me. Back then I had thrown hard—that's why they destroyed my pitching arm for a season.

But now I threw *hard*.

On game day, I had warmed up and was on the mound when the ringleader of my attackers came to the batter's box. He took his stance and was looking insolent. I was mad.

I threw my hardest fastball right at his rib cage. Back then, at 14, I was probably throwing about 85 miles per hour. I drilled him right in the ribs, and he hit the ground, writhing in pain.

But then I felt something I hadn't anticipated. I felt bad for taking him down like that.

I didn't have time to ponder that unexpected feeling. The fans knew about the Antimite guys jumping me. They also knew I had great ball control. So it was clear that my hitting the Antimite guy hadn't been an accident.

People were yelling in the stands, shoving each other; next thing I knew, the cops were there. They took up positions, and the game went on under their watch. Word came back that the hitter's ribs weren't broken, just badly bruised. When I went to bat, their pitcher tried to drill me but missed. He got thrown out of the game.

It was a zoo . . . but we won that game. I remember driving home, my dad's eyes watching in the rearview mirror of the Riviera, looking to see if we were being followed. We all watched my back from then on, and I felt I'd gotten a taste of revenge. The only problem was it wasn't as sweet as I'd thought it would be.

That spring was also the first time a Major League™ scout took a look at me. He was a scout for the Cincinnati Reds and was at a game watching his nephew play. He gave my parents his card and said he'd be keeping his eye on me. I was glad someone was.

So baseball turned my teenage hell at Damien High into a sort of purgatory . . . and then made my high school experience into something even better. Soon I was the freshman pitching a no-hitter against one of our big rivals, and then, eventually, my success on the mound overshadowed the horrible start I'd had at Damien. I was now outpitching Steve Schiro—the Goliath.

I was no longer the guy who had barfed his huge breakfast on the first day of Hell Week, or quit football after Flores knocked him out, or smeared CoverGirl and sweat all over his date at the first fall dance. My identity was set: I was Frank Pastore, pitcher.

8

★　★　★

REINVENTING MYSELF

Assuming a new identity came naturally to me. Remember, I was the kid who'd grown up in his own version of the Witness Protection Program.

I was helped in my "new me" quest by a few key developments. For one, thanks to the God who didn't exist, I'd grown about six inches and was no longer chubby. Second, my "mommy" wouldn't be taking me clothes shopping anymore. No longer would I wear the weird old-manish clothes she stole from her workplace.

No, I made the radical decision to buy my own clothes so I could finally look like all the other kids. Hang Ten shirts, colored T-shirts, Trek shoes, corduroys, sweatshirts, and Levi's. No more Vitalis and the wet look either. No more short hair. No more watching my language and speaking properly, like some rich kid with a silver spoon. I was going to cuss and use slang like everybody else. I was tired of being the geek who could throw stuff hard. I wanted to fit in, have friends, be liked, and maybe even be popular one day.

I didn't yet know who I really was, but it was dawning on me that I'd been living in a fake world. My life had been a facade. It was like having lived on a Hollywood set all your life and then finding out at

14 that the real world is a lot bigger. I wanted to explore the world and see how other people lived.

The more time I spent with friends' families, the more I realized how messed up my own family life was. But I didn't want anyone else to know. I wanted my friends to think I came from a normal background, just like theirs, where Mom and Dad actually looked at each other and maybe even kissed now and then, where friends came over to visit, and conversations were more than opportunities to heap shame, blame, and abuse on each other.

Mom had taught me well. I was really good at keeping up the facade that all was well at home. Faking a reality that didn't exist came quite naturally to me.

The confidence I'd gained on the baseball field had given me the entrée to become more outgoing. I looked like the other kids now and was even interested in doing well in school, since that was important to the popular kids. The funny social person who'd been inside me all along began to emerge.

I was known as a great baseball pitcher, and in spite of my weird upbringing, I seemed normal. People laughed when they were around me, and it was no longer at my expense. I started having friends. I even became more confident around girls . . . to the point that I actually started dating one of the popular cheerleaders. I was like a different person, and I was in control: I let my mom know I would hang out with whomever I wanted, and I'd be home whenever I wanted. I hated being at home. I slept there, but that was about it.

Then I made a discovery that was to change my life. Thanks to a gifted history teacher named Jim Steck, I learned that I had a mind. I had always thought of myself as an unlikely combination of uniquely brilliant and hopelessly stupid, thanks to my mom's weird input. I didn't have any real intellectual curiosity; I'd never learned to love to learn.

Mr. Steck's upper-level American history course was the coolest class in the high school. He made the Cold War, Watergate, Sino-American relations, and the other hot issues of the day intriguing and relevant. He was the toughest teacher in the school, and yet he was fair and knowledgeable. But most of all, he really cared about his students.

At the end of my freshman year, he teased me, "You don't have the guts to take my class, do you, Pastore?"

I had to prove him wrong, and so I took his class. He pushed me harder than any teacher ever had. His tests were killers. Every once in a while I'd get a paper back from him with "this is pretty good" noted on the top. I held on to those like baseball trophies.

I ended up taking more Steck classes than anybody ever had. Steck had an MA in history from USC, and he poured as much into us as he could. He became my surrogate father and older brother. He was my go-to guy for advice about girls, dating, life, college, career, friends, family, everything. He was the first person to speak truth into my life; I knew I could trust him. He showed me a view of myself that I'd never seen before, but I knew it was me. The *real* me.

With Mr. Steck's encouragement, I eventually even ran for vice president of the senior class . . . and won. It gets better. On the first day of senior year, we learned that the elected president had shoplifted some beer and gotten himself expelled over the summer. So I became senior class president, which was a pretty cool gig.

I loved Mr. Steck. Still do. Today he's an attorney, still in Upland, still helping kids.

Mr. Steck was present in my life in a way my dad was not. My dad was there physically—I saw him every night at home. But the two of us hardly talked after my sophomore year in high school. We didn't have anything in common, except baseball. Beyond that, there was no bond, no relationship. We were like two tenants in a boarding house run by my mother. Familiar strangers.

When spring of my sophomore year arrived, it was baseball season again, and it was the first time I got the chance to pitch to the best catcher in the whole valley in my age group, Johnny Pignotti. (The previous year I had been on the freshman team, while he'd played JV.)

The Pignottis were a legendary baseball family in our area. Mr. Pignotti always coached the best baseball teams. Johnny was part of "The Big Three," which also included Steve Schiro and Danny Monroe. My goal was to penetrate their group and render it "The Big Four." (Later, that would come true.)

The first time I visited Johnny's house, I took my mom's station wagon for a joy ride. I was 15 and didn't have a driver's license, but I didn't see that as a problem. Johnny met me at his front door, laughing while I gushed about how cool it was to drive.

I had been playing baseball with Johnny for a while and knew his dad from the ballpark. I heard his big voice boom from the den, "Frankie Pastore, how are ya?"

With that, I turned toward the den to say hi and then, like that scene in *The Godfather* when Michael Corleone first sees his true love, Apollonia, I was stunned.

There was this beautiful young girl with enormous brown eyes and long, thick brown hair, wearing a purple robe. She was sitting in a green chair doing homework, trying not to look at me.

"Hi, foxy!" I said to her.

She ignored me.

"Who's that?" I whispered to Johnny.

"Oh, that's just my little sister, Gina," he said.

"Hey!" I responded. "I didn't know you had a little sister!"

Johnny's dad got into the act, in classic Italian fashion.

"Gina!" he bellowed. "Say hi to Frankie Pastore!"

She smiled, her big brown eyes gazing right at me. "Hi," she said shyly.

The Pignottis were everything my family wasn't—authentic, unpretentious, relational, loud, and loving. Real. And miracle of miracles, Mrs. Pignotti actually cooked!

I had grown up in restaurants. My mother was a terrible cook. We ate out four nights a week, every week, every year, my whole life. The waitresses all knew my name. On our "home" nights we had TV dinners and big bowls of ice cream.

"Frankie!" Mr. Pignotti bellowed. "You hungry? Anna, fix Frankie a plate," he said to his wife. "Frankie, you gotta eat, you're a growing boy!"

Mrs. Pignotti had just cooked some pasta with homemade sauce, veal cutlets, and a huge salad with ripe tomatoes, crisp lettuce, and an oil-and-vinegar dressing with fresh-rubbed garlic. I was in heaven.

So it was no wonder that from that point on, I was at the Pignottis' house all the time. The food was the best I'd ever had. Mr. Pignotti had a garden, and we were eating the stuff he grew in his backyard. I thought that happened only on TV, not in Upland.

I started calling Mr. and Mrs. Pignotti "Mom" and "Dad" early on. I felt so at home with them. They were so normal, so American, so Italian. We'd watch ball games together, Mr. Pignotti pointing out all the inside baseball stuff, making sure I was learning how to pitch by watching what the big leaguers were doing—how they were setting up the hitters and pitching to their defense, when they needed a strikeout or a double play.

One evening as I was leaving and kissing "Mom" good-bye, little Gina suddenly piped up. "One day I'm going to marry you, Frankie Pastore!" she proclaimed.

We all stared at her and then laughed. So cute. She was only 11.

But Gina wasn't laughing. She was just smiling, looking at me as if she knew something I didn't. I can still remember those eyes . . .

9

★ ★ ★

DREAMS COME TRUE

Fast-forward to three years later. I was almost 18 and had
morphed from ye olde marshmallow to one of those high school
golden guys. I was the popular athlete, the senior class prez who dated
a trophy cheerleader, the guy who got the academic scholarship to
Stanford University, and one of the top high school pitchers in the
country.

It was May 1975. Johnny was having a graduation party at his
house. I got there late. The house was packed with people, and KC
and the Sunshine Band was blaring on the patio.

I had signed a letter of intent to Stanford, one of just two full-
rides they offered that year. The Major League Baseball™ draft was
a week away, and there was talk I would go in the first round. I was a
free man since my cheerleader girlfriend and I were currently on the
outs, and I was on the prowl. Life at the top was good. I was a lifetime
away from the nerdy horrors of my freshman year.

I was walking into Johnny's house through the garage. Standing
in the doorway at the top step into the house, was Johnny's little sister, Gina. She was only 13, but she looked much older. I'd never
seen her wearing makeup. I'd gotten over my Appollonia moment
when I'd first seen her, though I'd been teasing her for a couple of

years, telling her I wished she was older so we could go out. But as far as I was concerned, it was all talk, and she'd gotten over her crush on me.

"Hi, Gina," I said. "You look great!"

I went up the stairs and leaned over to kiss her on the cheek. To my shock, she turned her head to kiss me on the lips. And it wasn't just a friendly peck. It was electric, romantic. Surprising.

But come on, I thought. *I've just graduated high school, and she's going into the eighth grade!*

The kiss went on much longer than I'd expected. When we finally pulled back, I looked into Gina's beautiful face and saw, for the first time, the man I was in her eyes. The man I wanted to become.

Then someone came barreling through the door, and the moment was broken.

A few days later, the Cincinnati Reds drafted me in the second round. I was the third high school pitcher selected in the nation. The reps showed up at our house, contract in hand, and even though it was a dream come true, there was a stubborn streak inside of me. Maybe it had been planted there by Mr. Steck, who didn't like the dark side of professional sports and wanted me to go straight to college.

I'd been recruited by various universities to play ball for them, including UCLA and USC, but when I visited those campuses, I felt as if the coaches were arrogant. They seemed to have the attitude, "Well, of course you're coming here. What idiot would even *consider* going anywhere else?"

So I wanted to go to Stanford.

But now the pros had come calling. So here I was with the Cincinnati Reds in my kitchen, offering me major bucks to join the team, and I was telling them I wanted to go to school instead.

"Are you crazy?" the Reds' scouting director sputtered. "This is the largest bonus in Reds history! It's twice what we gave Johnny Bench when we signed him!"

It was fifty thousand dollars.

Keep in mind that this was 1975. Professional baseball and the pro athletes' salaries were completely different back then. And I was just 17 years old, so $50K sounded pretty good to me. I could buy a new stereo and lots of other stuff, as well as my dream car, a brand-new Datsun 280Z.

So I made what would become my usual default: an impulsive decision. Later I'd discover that since I had no real foundation and my mother had constantly sprung life-changing decisions on me without warning, I had a tendency to do major capricious things without much consideration. But back then, of course, I had no interest in self-examination. I had an interest in doing what I wanted to do at the moment.

"Okay!" I told the Reds' reps. "I'm in!"

I was under 18, so I needed a parent to sign for me. Mom was there, wearing a smelly muumuu and chain-smoking like a fiend. She didn't want me to play baseball professionally. She wanted me to go to college, since she never did. Meanwhile, my dad wanted me to play pro ball, since he never did. I guess my mom felt she'd lose their tug-of-war if I did what my dad wanted me to do. She refused to sign the documents.

That made me all the more determined to go with the Reds.

So the reps and I jumped into their rental car and drove down to the plant where my dad was working. He came out of the factory, and right there in the parking lot, on the hood of that hot rental Buick, he signed my first professional baseball contract. Tears were running down his cheeks. He was so proud that he couldn't speak.

On the way home, the reps took me to the Rawlings warehouse, where we picked up a couple of baseball gloves and three pairs of cleats. I would be on my way to Billings, Montana, in three days, where the Reds' lowest-level minor-league team was based.

I arrived in Billings, 17 years old and filled with dreamy expectations of what professional baseball was all about. I checked into the Northern Hotel. Our players' rate there was five dollars a day. That might have been too much. I felt trapped without a car. I barely slept that first night away from home. I got up early, ate breakfast, and took a cab to the ballpark.

I was the first player there. I found my locker with my name on the card above it and set my bag, with my new gloves and cleats in it, down on the dirty floor. An old guy straight out of Central Casting, Baseball Division, came around the corner and told me to go get a hat and then "sign the d— baseballs" that were on a table.

Jauntily wearing my new red Billings Mustangs hat, I set out to autograph six dozen new baseballs that would be given to VIPs. I'd never signed a ball before. So I just picked what looked like the best place and signed away. Other players started drifting in, banging their lockers, and signing the balls. I had no idea why they were glaring at me.

After we were all done, the manager, Jimmy Hoff, gathered up the balls and took them into his office. About four seconds later we all heard a string of expletives, and then he yelled my name:

"Pastore! Get in here!"

It was just like getting called into the principal's office. Everyone was staring at me. I slithered into Hoff's office.

"Who do you think you are?" he yelled. "That'll cost you $25!"

I had no idea what he was talking about, but since I was running my own finances, $25 was a lot of money for me.

"What?" I sputtered.

Hoff looked at me as if I were from outer space. "Kid," he said, "you ever sign a baseball before?"

"No," I replied.

"Well, here's the deal," he said. He jabbed his beefy finger where I'd grandly signed my name. "*This* is where the manager signs the ball. That would be me. You signed in my spot! You ever do that again, and you are outta here! Forever!"

I walked out of Hoff's office, and the older guys were all laughing. By older, I mean they were 21 or 22 and had played together at the big schools, like USC, Florida State, Texas. They knew the ropes. And here I was, age 17, the new kid in school . . . seventh-grade geek all over again.

After morning calisthenics, the regulars went off to take batting practice, and the pitchers and catchers went down to the right-field corner bull pen. About 20 of us sat in the grass, listening to the minor-league pitching instructor, Scott Breeden, and Jimmy Hoff, the manager whom I'd already offended, lay down the dos and don'ts. We all knew who got drafted when, and we all wanted to see how good the guys were who got drafted ahead of us. It was pecking-order time. Time to find out where you were on the food chain.

Tony Moretto, the first-round pick, was this left-handed hitter from Indiana who had hit something like .600 in high school. He had an almost flawless swing. The ball cracked off his bat and into outer space . . . and he was only 18. We were all impressed. And here

I was, the second-round pick, the loser who had signed the balls in the wrong place.

There were two mounds in the bull pen. I got on one, and Hoff threw me the first ball. The second ball went to this huge six-foot-six animal from Lake Charles, Louisiana. His nickname was Gator. He wrestled alligators for fun. He set the high school state record in the javelin, and rumor had it that though he had never played organized baseball before, the Reds had drafted him in the fourth round for his crazy arm.

As I got loose, I was hitting my spots, throwing pretty hard. Gator was firing wildly. He didn't really have any kind of a windup. He just reared back and fired, as if he were throwing a javelin. His fastball was literally going 100 miles per hour, but it was all over the place. Guys were running for cover.

About 20 fastballs into it, I made the up-down sign with my closed glove and announced "curve ball" to Mark Miller, the star high school catcher. I snapped off a few pretty good hooks. They were breaking just right, and I was feeling pretty good.

Meanwhile, Gator was firing bullets next to me, all over the place. Birds were falling from the sky. He jabbed me in the shoulder.

"Hey," he said, "gimme that curve ball."

I wasn't sure what he meant, but I wasn't going to mess with Gator. We exchanged baseballs.

He looked it over and then hollered to his catcher, "Curve ball!"

Gator proceeded to throw a screaming fastball that glanced off the top of the catcher's mask, knocking him backward. The catcher never got a glove on it, which was good, since it would have broken his hand. The ball crashed like a meteorite into the fence about 12 feet behind the plate, shattering the wood.

The catcher rolled over and lifted his mask. We could see that his face was frozen and white. Here he'd been expecting a curve ball and almost got his face torn off by a fastball traveling at the speed of sound. We were all stunned—Gator included.

He'd thought that if he used my curve ball, the ball would break on its own.

10

★ ★ ★

STANFORD MAN IS NO CURRY FAN

I returned home from my adventures in Billings in September 1975. My mom had deposited the first half of my bonus—$17,500 after taxes—in her account, since I didn't have one yet.

I couldn't wait to spend that money.

One of my best friends in high school, Jorge Gomez, had a 240Z. I loved that car. I had my mom drive me over to the local Datsun dealer. I'd seen pictures of the new 280Z in car magazines, and when I walked into the dealership, there, in the center of the showroom floor, was this gorgeous, sleek car. It was persimmon. Not red. Red was ordinary. Persimmon was cool.

A salesman came up to us, looking down his nose at me and not liking my muumuu mother much more.

"May I help you?" he asked in a tone that let us know we were wasting his precious time.

"Yes," I said. "I want to buy this car."

His eyebrows went up, and he turned to my mother.

"No," I said. "*I'm* buying it. Cash."

We went back to his grand office, which was a little gray cubicle, and I peeled off $7,200 in $100 bills. Then I drove my persimmon Z . . . straight to the Pignottis' house.

Now that I had wheels, it was time to game the system the way I'd seen my mom do it a thousand times. I'd signed with the Cincinnati Reds, but I still had that academic scholarship to Stanford, and the papers to prove it. Since it wasn't a sports scholarship, I didn't see why Stanford would mind that I'd done a little thing like sign with the Reds. The university wanted me for my brains, right? So they should be glad to see me.

Two weeks later, I hopped in my Z late one night and drove north on the 101, rocking to my Bad Company eight-track. I arrived at Stanford in the early morning, feeling good. My name was still listed at the new-student registration desk, and the cute girl there gave me my dorm assignment.

I got to my dorm and walked into my room. There was Bob, my university-assigned roommate, tokin' on a bong and jamming to Jefferson Starship. Bob was feeling mellow and took to me pretty well. I gently explained that I was a player for the Cincinnati Reds and that they were pretty stringent about things like, uh, drugs. After I explained what *stringent* meant, Bob was on board with me. He kindly agreed not to smoke dope in our room anymore and wafted gently out into the hall.

I unloaded my stuff and headed to the gym to register for classes and get my textbooks, which weighed a ton. I got in the scholarship line when it was time to pay.

When I reached the front of the line, I announced proudly, "Frank Pastore, academic."

The girl at the desk fanned through some papers and then went to look for her boss.

He arrived at the table, took me to the side, and pronounced sentence: "Mr. Pastore, I'm sorry to inform you, but because you've signed a professional baseball contract with the Cincinnati Reds, your financial-need factor has changed, and your scholarship has been revoked."

Today I look back and wonder just why this came as a surprise at the time. But back then, the world pretty well revolved around me, and I had thought Stanford and the Reds and I would all be one happy family. I kept staring at the scholarship guy like I was mentally impaired. Maybe I'd inhaled too much of Roommate Bob's second-hand smoke.

"Mr. Pastore?" said the registration guy.

I came out of my fog and made another impulsive decision.

"Okay," I said brightly. "No problem! I'll just pay my full tuition out of my pocket!"

In an instant this whole college thing changed from "Ain't it cool to go to a big-name university for free?" to "I'm paying for this, so it better be worth every nickel!"

So I was dissatisfied that I had some teaching assistant teaching my history class instead of the big-name professor. I was upset that there were 200 students in Econ 101. I didn't like my hippy-dippy sociology professor. I was frustrated with Roommate Bob, who always had druggies in the room. I didn't like that my new car was sitting in student parking and could be vandalized at any moment.

And I was upset I was paying for all this out of my own wallet.

I signed up to work in the kitchen at Lagunita Court—my dorm—doing dishes. About two weeks into the semester, we were serving chicken curry on a Friday night. I had a busy weekend of study planned. My first economics exam was on Monday, and I also had a long English paper due that day. I hadn't even started it. Since I worked in the kitchen, I ate for free. I didn't even like chicken curry, but hey, it was free, so I ate it. A lot of it.

That night at about 10 o'clock, I walked down the dorm hallway to go to the bathroom. A guy was throwing up in the stall. He didn't look like one of the druggies, so it caught my eye.

I went back to the room and realized I wasn't feeling too good either. I raced to the bathroom, kicked open the stall, and started throwing up next to the first guy. There was another guy in the third stall. We were all heaving our guts out.

The next thing I remember, I was opening my eyes in a hospital room. Actually, it was the infirmary. A nurse came in and told me that I'd been sleeping all weekend. It was Monday. I'd gotten food poisoning from the chicken curry. Everyone who ate it at Lagunita that night had gotten it too.

Great. I had missed my econ exam, hadn't done my English paper, had thrown up my guts, and didn't like Stanford very much. You guessed it: I made another impulsive decision.

"I'm outta here!" I decided.

I wobbled over to the Dean of Students' office and laid out my plight.

"Well, Frank," he said graciously. "It just so happens that today is the last day for a tuition refund. But I can't do anything about the books. If baseball doesn't turn out, just know, once you're accepted at Stanford, you're always accepted. You can come back anytime."

He told me he'd take care of the paperwork and mail the refund to my parents' house. I headed back to the dorm, waved through the smoke to Roommate Bob, and packed up my stuff. Within two hours I'd hopped in the Z and was toolin' south on the 101, chillin' to Jethro Tull.

11

★ ★ ★

REAL MEN

So I was no longer a Stanford man. I was Frank Pastore, minor-league pitcher, Cincinnati Reds. I was ready to bond with my baseball brethren, no matter what it took, and embrace "baseball player" as my sole identity.

Fitting in and being accepted didn't come easily. Back in Billings, I had to first pass a crucial test. You already know about good old Gator of "Gimme the curve ball" fame. On my first day in Billings, after the workout, he called over to me.

"Hey, Frank," he drawled. "Ever chew tobacco?"

All eyes turned to me.

"Sure," I lied.

"Ever dip?" asked Gator.

"Nope," I confessed.

"Well, if you were a real man," he said, "you'd just take a little pinch between your cheek and gum, like this." He packed a wad into his lower lip.

Then he extended his can of Skoal to me.

This may sound like a bunch of junior-high boys in the locker room, but some things just never change about guys. There was a lot of testosterone in the air. A lot of attitude. All I had to do was chew some tobacco. How bad could it be?

With all the nonchalance I could muster, I opened the can, took a healthy pinch, and put it inside my lower lip. Life was great for about two minutes. Then the room started to spin, I got clammy, my stomach churned, and I ran for the bathroom and spewed my guts out.

All the guys were laughing their heads off, rolling on the clubhouse floor. I was glad I could provide them so much joy.

But as sick as I was, I wasn't going down. I washed the vomit off my face and marched right back into that clubhouse.

"Gimme the can," I said to Gator. The guys couldn't believe it. He just grinned and handed it over.

Every molecule in my body screamed at me to stop. I ignored them all, packed another dip inside my lip, and through an exercise of mind over matter, didn't heave again.

So began my great love affair with tobacco. I went on over the years to do every form of tobacco known to man: dip, chew, snuff, plug, leaf, pipe, cigars, cigarettes, filtered and unfiltered, regular, menthol, and the very best chew of my life—homemade peach-leaf tobacco in Atlanta, courtesy of Johnny Bench.

I became an avid dipper. I was told that you would get lip cancer only if you regularly slept with Copenhagen in your mouth. I knew plenty of guys who did that, but I was a Skoal guy. Copenhagen smelled like horse manure to me.

They say that chewing tobacco and snuff contain 28 cancer-causing agents, including things like arsenic and formaldehyde. They say that Babe Ruth died from a tumor in the back of his throat, a result of chewing, and outfielder Bill Tuttle, who always posed for his baseball cards with a big chaw in his cheek, developed an enormous tumor that caused him to lose most of his face before he died.

But of course I didn't care about all that. I was young and invincible. So I started pitching with a chaw. It worked well for me: Levi Garrett tobacco and a couple big pieces of watermelon bubble gum. You had to wrap it just right, chewing up the gum first, then wadding your chew—with all its nice arsenic and formaldehyde—into a little ball, then grabbing the tip of the gum and pulling it out into a thin string, turning the ball as you covered the chew with the strings of gum.

I became a legendary spitter. Deadly within 10 feet. I could hit guys' shoe tips from a good distance without getting their laces wet. We'd set up a Dixie cup on the dugout stairs; you got one point for hitting the cup and two points for getting it inside the cup. I usually won.

Of course, when we weren't on the field or in the dugout, we were gentlemanly about using a spittoon. It was pretty classless and gross to use a transparent container, like a water glass or a clear plastic cup. On the baseball buses and planes, we used soft-drink cans.

Toward the end of my rookie year, on a 12-hour bus trip, I made the mistake every chewer fears most. It was about three o'clock in the morning. The card games were over, and some of the smaller guys had climbed up into the luggage rack to sleep. A few guys had their reading lights on. I was dozing, but I had my Skoal. My Coke-can spittoon was propped in the empty seat next to me. My Coke to drink was between my legs.

We hit a bump. It woke me enough to rewad my jacket pillow a little bit and to realize that I was thirsty. I reached for my Coke and downed a big swig. I went from half-asleep to DEFCON 1 in a nanosecond. And if you draw nothing else from this book, the message I have for you is this: *Never* drink your own spit.

Aside from that life-message, which of course didn't deter me from my mad love affair with tobacco, there isn't much I can report from all my many miles on team bus trips. Not much that is printable in a family-friendly book, I mean.

There's nothing like all-night rides on a bus full of baseball players, pulling into the Wendy's drive-through at about midnight and saying, "Yes, we'd like 80 double cheeseburgers, 40 large fries, and 40 diet drinks."

The little middle infielders and the greyhound outfielders would be up in the luggage racks. The poker players were in the back of the bus playing on a cardboard box with a towel over it in the aisle outside the bathroom. The readers were up front where it was a little quieter and people didn't get mad about the lights.

And, aah, the music. My baseball days were way before iPods, even before the Sony Walkman. We had the real thing, man. Remember those gigantic ghetto blasters that ran on eight double-D batteries and weighed a ton?

You could tell what kind of music a guy liked just by asking him where he liked to sit on the bus. Country was up front for the manager and coaches, rock was in the middle, and then as you moved to the back of the bus, you traveled through what we now call "urban," all the way to Caribbean in the far back. After a big win, we'd break out the disco or jam to KC and the Sunshine Band; Earth, Wind, and Fire; or Aerosmith.

Some of our best times took place off the bus. One night when I was playing for the Nashville Sounds, in 1978, we were on a road trip to Charlotte, North Carolina. I heard a soft knock at my hotel-room door. It was Bobby Mayer, a left-handed pitcher from Florida State, who had just joined the team. He was gathering a few of the guys together; he said he had something "really special" to show us. I thought it better be pretty special, since it was two o'clock in the morning.

About a dozen of us quietly followed Bobby up and out onto the roof of the hotel. There he displayed what would become the infamous Three Man Water Balloon Launcher. All I saw was a bunch of surgical tubing, a funnel that you'd use to pour oil into your car engine, and a wastebasket full of water balloons about the size of baseballs. But then a couple of the guys helped him set it up: It was, of course, a giant slingshot.

Bobby scoped out his targets far below. There were some ladies of the night five stories down and about two blocks away, hanging out in front of a bar. Two guys grabbed either end of the surgical tubing and began slowly walking forward, each with an upstretched arm as stiff as he could lock it, to form the two uprights of the slingshot.

Meanwhile, Bobby, the launcher, sat on his butt pulling back on the funnel that held the first water balloon. Bobby gave the countdown: three . . . two . . . one. The first projectile launched . . . and flew through the air like a missile. (Well, it *was* a missile.) It soared about 150 yards . . . just 50 yards too short of our new friends on the street.

We reloaded, stretched the tubing to about 15 feet, and launched again. This time the balloon crashed open on the sidewalk next to the hookers. They jumped, freaked, and looked around . . . but saw no one.

We shot about six more missiles before their pimp arrived. Now, since it was mano a mano, or actually men-o a pimp-o, we fired again and hit his car. He would have killed us if he could have gotten to us.

We thought we were hidden from street view since we were launching behind a big billboard sign on top of the hotel. But when the pimp's outstretched arm pointed to the top of our building, we realized that the billboard hadn't covered all of us. We hadn't noticed that our legs, from the knees down, were in plain sight. So when the pimp looked up, he saw 24 legs beneath the billboard.

He hopped in his car, hung a fast U-turn, and headed for our hotel. We panicked. There were loaded water balloons everywhere. We all scrambled to our rooms as fast as we could. We absolutely knew this guy had a gun, and he was going to blow us away, one by one by one.

The long night passed . . . and we were still alive.

Our fear of angry pimps, not to mention our manager, didn't stop us from practical joking whenever we could get away with it. We'd put thermalgesic ointment, aka "hot stuff," in armpits of undershirts and in jocks, so that when a fellow player would start sweating, he'd *really* start sweating. Or we'd snip shoelaces just enough so they'd suddenly break when a guy yanked to tie them, and he'd get fined a dollar a minute for being late to batting practice. And, of course, the shaving cream in the ear part of the phone when a guy's wife was calling the clubhouse, the rubber snake in the locker bit, and late-night wake-up calls.

But the greatest joy of all for me and the rest of the grown-up boys came when I was playing for the Reds. It might have been the greatest sports prank of all time, immortalized by George Plimpton in his book *Paper Lion*. The first time I saw it was in the Reds' Tampa clubhouse in 1978.

Along with the rest of the rookies, I was excited when we were all told that a live mongoose was being delivered to the clubhouse all the way from India. For days, the veterans had been asking Bernie, our clubby, when it would be arriving.

"Oh, it's still going through customs in Miami. It should be here any day," he'd say.

We could hardly contain ourselves, but of course we wanted to be cool about it. Still, our expectation was at a fever pitch when Bernie announced that the mongoose had arrived in the night. But we had to be very quiet, he explained; it was sleeping in the laundry room.

Pretty soon, Angel Torres, this wonderful little left-hander from the Dominican Republic—nicknamed Chivo because he could do a spot-on imitation of a goat—asked Bernie if he could take a look. Bernie said he didn't want to spook the mongoose. But then the other vets all gathered around, telling him he should let Chivo see it . . . and eventually Bernie reluctantly agreed.

"Only if you guys are really quiet," he cautioned. "It had a hard trip, and I don't want to get it excited. When it wakes up, it'll be really hungry, and when it's hungry, it's angry, and when it's angry, it'll attack anything. Man, you ought to see how quick this thing is. You know it kills cobras, right? So, yeah, you can see it for a second, but only if you promise to be quiet."

"We promise," we all said, with Chivo in the lead.

By now, the whole team was in on it, slowly following the rookies into the laundry room.

"Shhh, careful now," Bernie said.

We all walked silently over to the table with a large white shower towel draped over a big box. Bernie carefully peeled back the towel to reveal a metal cage with "DANGER" stenciled on the sides. It was about three feet long, two feet wide, and about a foot tall. It had wire mesh covering part of the end.

In a barely audible whisper, Bernie breathed, "Oh, it's sleeping. Shhh, come look. Be quiet, though."

He bent down to peer inside the opening behind the mesh. We could see just a little bit of a furry tail and a water dish. We assumed it must have been asleep in the darkness of the covered area, with only its tail visible.

Chivo bent down to see, as did about six of us, but Chivo was the primary target. When his face was about six inches from the mesh, Bernie released a spring-loaded lever on the side of the box. The mesh popped open, and the huge, furry tail exploded out of the box directly onto Chivo's chest, inches from his throat. He started screaming wildly in Spanish, flailing in panic at the mongoose tail, which was now stuck to his shirt.

The veterans were rolling on the floor, laughing so hard they were crying. Chivo was still beating at the tail on his chest, not yet realizing that the mongoose had no body, just a tail, which was in fact a fake tail that stuck to his shirt because it had Velcro backing. The rest of us were laughing too, out of sheer gratitude to God that we hadn't been the rookie targeted for the infamous Cincinnati Reds Great Mongoose Prank.

Yeah, the baseball life was guy heaven sometimes, like camp for grown-up boys. All it needed was women. There were plenty of them on the road, of course, and I regularly took advantage of their availability. Then I went home to Upland one Thanksgiving to take little Gina Pignotti out on her very first official date . . . and everything changed.

12

★　★　★

JOHNNY'S LITTLE SISTER

I had always promised Gina that I would be the one to take her out on her very first date, when she turned 15. She was a freshman at St. Lucy's Priory High School for girls, and it was Thanksgiving evening, 1976. I had dated around in my two years in the minor leagues but had had no serious relationships. I didn't date girls for relationships. I went out with cheerleaders, groupies, and aspiring models. For sex.

But Gina was only 15, so there was nothing sexual, romantic, or anything else intended when I picked her up to go to the movies. We went to the local theater, with a choice of either *Bambi* or *Shampoo*. The first was the rereleased Disney classic, as innocent as they come, except for the terrible part when Bambi's mother dies. I was prepared to comfort Gina when we got to that part, because I knew she'd pick *Bambi*. Despite the passionate kiss she had given me two years previously, I was still thinking of her as "Johnny's little sister." So I was surprised when she picked *Shampoo*, starring Warren Beatty as a hairdresser who relentlessly slept with his female customers. *Shampoo* was R-rated, but since I was over 18, an alleged adult, Gina could see it. We walked into the theater holding hands. I thought it was cute.

Afterward, I wanted to get her home as soon as I politely could, since I wanted to go out to the clubs and look for some real action. So I took her to our local diner for a hamburger, thinking we'd be there for about an hour, and then I could get on with the evening.

We sat in the restaurant for three hours. We talked and talked about everything. It was so easy, so comfortable, so natural. I loved the effortless conversation without all the sexual tension. It was the best date I'd ever been on. I took her home and softly kissed her good night at her front door.

Then I went home.

After that, we started talking on the phone all the time. I was constantly over at the Pignottis' home, not to see Johnny anymore—he was away at college anyway—but to spend time with Gina. We'd watch TV and laugh and talk for hours. We'd eat dinner with Mom and Dad Pignotti. It was like being in the home I'd never had, but with something new.

Meanwhile, my parents had moved again, but they weren't much of a presence in my life anyway. Mr. Pignotti was more of a dad than my own father. When I had a bad game or needed encouragement or advice, Mr. Pignotti was there for me.

During the following off-season, Gina invited me to her Christmas formal. Here I was, this 20-year-old, worldly guy taking this 16-year-old sophomore to her dance. It was raining, and I didn't have an umbrella. Gina's thick, brown, wavy hair got as wet as if she'd just stepped out of the shower. She was upset, but I thought she looked absolutely beautiful.

At the dance the chaperones thought I was a chaperone because I looked so old. Gina's friends thought it was cool that she was dating a professional baseball player, while the other girls were cooing over the varsity starters in high school.

We just laughed. She didn't care that I was a baseball player. She didn't care what I did, really. She cared about who I was. With Gina, I could take off the layers and facades I always wore. I don't want to sound pseudo-psychological, but what happened was this: As I was getting to know Gina, she gave me the freedom, for the first time in my life, to begin to get to know myself.

You have to remember that this was in olden times, so we had no cell phones, no texting, no instant communications. We actually wrote each other letters every day when we were apart. We splurged and called each other once a week, on Sunday nights. When we were together, it was as if we were in our own special zone. Time stood still . . . or zoomed at three times its normal rate. I couldn't stand being apart from her.

One Sunday we were out and stopped at Tiffany's Coffee Shop. We sat in a booth across from each other, and I slid my hand slowly across the table to envelop hers. I looked into those dark brown eyes, brought her hands to my lips, and kissed them.

"Gina," I said, "I'm in love with you. I want to marry you. I want to have a family with you. Will you marry me?"

She held my hand and looked deep into my eyes. "Frank," she whispered, "I love you, too!"

13

★ ★ ★

MOM'S TRUE LOVE: A BOY NAMED DUDE

Soon after Gina and I declared what was already so clear in our hearts, I drove off to Tampa for my first year of spring training with the Big Red Machine. I was going to be in the clubhouse with guys I had watched on TV as a kid. I was thrilled.

When I wasn't thinking about baseball, my mind was on Gina. I wanted her to be there with me. But that would have to wait. After all, she was only 16.

On the first day of big-league camp, I was playing catch with somebody and accidentally threw the ball over the guy's head. It drilled Sparky Anderson, the Reds' Hall of Fame manager, right in the calf. Hard.

Sparky hobbled for a moment, took his roster sheet out of his uniform back pocket, grabbed a pen, and signaled with his hand for me to turn around so he could see my number. I did and then watched him draw a line through a name and grimace at me. I pitched one inning in a meaningless game and was the first pitcher sent down to the minors.

That spring I made the AAA club as the fifth starter. But I didn't pitch well, and the arrival of an unexpected visitor didn't help. My

dad showed up at the park about a month into the season, unan-
nounced. Crying. Mom had filed for divorce, kicked him out of the
house, and he had driven his Riviera from LA to be with me. He had
nowhere else to go. Mom was selling the house and moving back
"home," which somehow meant her childhood home of Birmingham.
She was sending the divorce papers to Dad care of my ball club.

So here I was, trying to concentrate on pitching in AAA, and
this stranger—my dad—was living in my apartment, crying all the
time. I didn't know what to do with him. It seemed to me that getting free of my mom was a good thing. I couldn't conceive why he was
so upset and helpless.

My dad stayed two weeks, just enough time to totally blow my
concentration. I got sent down to the Nashville Sounds; I sent Dad
back to LA.

In Nashville I was back with my friends. I did well, got my mojo
back, and then my mother showed up out of nowhere. She wasn't
wearing her usual muumuu. She was actually dressed up, looking better than I'd ever seen her look. She appeared at the ballpark an hour
before game time. And she wasn't alone. She was hanging all over
some guy I'd never seen before.

"Frankie," she said proudly, "I want you to meet the man I've
always loved. This is the man who should have been your father . . .
This is Dude!"

Dude?

I'm a verbal guy, but I was speechless. Evidently this "dude" had
been the dreamboat my mother had told me about. She'd eloped with
him when she was 17. Her dad had had the marriage annulled, and
my mother had run away from Birmingham to California. She now
told me she had been seeing Dude throughout her four marriages,

that he was the real father of my stepsister—which would have been news to husband number three—and that it was only right that they be together now in their golden years.

We went out to dinner, just like normal people would. I sat in the restaurant, unable to eat. My mother was sitting at the table, all over Dude, French-kissing him, running her hands through his thinning hair. I'd never seen my parents even hold hands. I'd never seen them kiss on the lips. This Dude thing was so wrong, on so many levels, that I was just about catatonic.

I guess Mom was recapturing the shabby magic of her lost youth. She was oblivious to everything but making out with Dude, and Dude was grinning like somebody who'd won the lottery. Maybe he was on drugs.

They warmly invited me to come live with them in Birmingham after the baseball season was over.

Right.

Perhaps it was fitting when, a few weeks later, I sprained my finger after diving into second base. My *middle* finger on my right hand. It was taped to a splint in a rather rude position, and it sort of summed up how I was feeling.

But all that mattered to me at this point was going home to the only person who kept life sane. Gina. She was still only 16, but we'd made our plans.

We were going to elope.

14

★ ★ ★

ROBERT LUDLUM WOULD HAVE BEEN PROUD

I had already been miserable without Gina, even before my mother's Dude episode, which left me reeling. I thought about Gina constantly. I watched the other players with their young wives, and I ached for her. In spring training we decided that I'd ask her dad for her hand in marriage. Maybe getting her parents' approval, setting a date, and making it official would make our time apart more bearable.

So, when I picked up the phone to make my regularly scheduled Sunday-night phone call to her house, my heart was thudding in my chest as I heard her dad's voice on the other end of the line.

"Hi, Dad!" I said.

"Frankie!" he responded warmly, as he always did. "How ya doin'?"

"Dad, I, uh, need to talk to you about something important," I stammered.

"Do you need help?" he asked immediately. "Are you okay?"

"No, no, I'm fine," I said. "It's about Gina and me."

Mr. Pignotti suddenly knew where I was going. "Yeah?"

"Well, I want to marry Gina," I said.

"Oh, Frankie," he responded. "I know that. But she's so young now. You'll have plenty of time for that later. Right now what you need to do is just focus on baseball."

"But, Dad," I came back. "We love each other! I love her, and I'm asking your permission for us to be engaged."

He could tell by my tone of voice that this was a lot more serious than he had imagined.

"Frankie! She's only 16 years old! And you're what—20, 21? No. No. She's too young. Focus on baseball right now, and you can be together all you want when you get back home."

"But, Dad—" I started, and then he cut me off.

"Okay, Frankie," he said. "I'll talk to you later."

Then I could hear him hollering for his daughter. "Gina! GEEE-NAHHHH!"

That was it. Dad had said no, which only made me more determined than ever. At that instant I knew I wasn't going to wait another 27 months for her to graduate from high school.

Gina got on the phone.

"Hi, baby," I said. "Go back in the bedroom so we can talk . . . and shut the door."

When she got back on the line, I continued. "Gina, I love you. I love you more than anything, and being apart is killing me. I can't wait two more years. I don't even want to wait one more year. Sweetheart, let's elope as soon as this season is over."

There was a pause. Gina and her mother hadn't been getting along since she and I had started getting serious. Her mom had been thrilled at first about us dating; now she was super-critical and angry with Gina all the time. They fought constantly. Gina was ready to get away.

"Are you sure?" she asked. "Do you really want to do this?"

"Yeah, honey," I responded, having made up my mind somewhere between the time when her dad started hollering for her to get on the phone and when she picked up.

"Let's do it. Let's be together."

"Okay," she said. "I love you, too. I miss you so much; I wish you were here right now."

That only made the ache that much more painful.

I spent the next five months scratching out the details of how we were going to pull this off. I was a huge Robert Ludlum spy novel fan; I applied the clandestine operations tips I had learned from his books into our elopement strategy.

We were to tell no one. Gina wouldn't be able to store anything at a friend's house. She'd have to leave the house on Elopement Day with only what could fit into a brown paper bag, since a suitcase would be an obvious tip-off.

We'd buy her new clothes, shoes, makeup, and a curling iron when we got to the safe house. We wouldn't make any traceable credit-card transactions. I'd close out my bank account at Chino Valley Bank at the last possible moment, since Gina's dad knew everybody at the bank. I would forge her baptismal record to show she was 18. I had practice at this, since I'd forged fake IDs for my friends in high school so we could go to bars.

Gina and I would get the blood tests done midmorning when it would look least suspicious. We'd pay cash for the wedding bands. I would book three flights out of Ontario International Airport, the closest one to Gina's home in Upland. One would be to Acapulco, another to Hawaii, and another to Orlando—all in my real name. The real flight would be a direct flight out of Los Angeles International Airport to Birmingham, under two aliases that were randomly chosen so they couldn't be traced.

Since my car would be in Nashville, our wheels would be my dad's 1963 Buick Riviera. We'd have to stay off the radar screen for about two weeks so that we could say the marriage had been consummated, that we were okay, and that we just wanted to be left alone. After that, we'd be easy to find. I'd start Instructional League in Tampa in October.

Bottom line, we hoped that her dad wouldn't put a Mob contract out on me and that the Reds wouldn't cancel my baseball contract.

I injured a finger on my pitching hand, and that circumstance allowed me to leave the team before the season ended. In late August, I flew from Nashville to LAX. We planned the Elopement Day for Thursday, August 31, 1978. It was Gina's first day of her junior year in high school. I rolled up to the house about 6:45 AM and walked into the kitchen to find Dad in his chair at the table reading the paper after making breakfast for the family.

"Geee-nahhh," he bellowed, suspecting nothing. "Frankie's here!"

Gina came down the hall dressed in her school uniform, carrying a brown paper bag.

"What's in the bag?" Dad asked.

"My PE clothes," said my lovely bride-to-be.

"Okay," he said, "you'd better not be late!"

"Bye, Dad," Gina said as she leaned over to kiss her father good-bye.

"Bye, Mom," she called down the hallway, as Mom didn't usually get up in the morning to see the kids off to school.

We hopped in my dad's Riviera and headed to the apartment so Gina could change out of her Catholic school uniform, which probably wouldn't go over well with the justice of the peace. I grabbed my already-packed suitcase.

We wanted to be first in line to pick up our marriage license at the county office in Upland. With all the documentation in hand, including our three-day-wait blood test and Gina's forged baptismal certificate, we were at the window when it slid open at eight o'clock.

Like a counterfeiter passing bad bills, I may have looked calm, cool, and collected on the outside, but inside, my heart was racing. The license fee was $7.50. I handed the clerk a $20, accepted her congratulations, and we raced off to the county offices in Colton, about 20 miles east on Interstate 10, to get married by a justice of the peace.

We were on a tight schedule. Our flight would leave LAX at 12:40 PM. We arrived at the little courthouse in Colton a few minutes before it opened at nine. The doors opened, and there were just four of us there—Gina and me and the judge and his assistant. The judge was friendly, chatty, genuinely interested in this young couple who wanted to get married with no witnesses in the middle of nowhere.

We didn't want to slip up and reveal too much, so I told him we had a flight to catch, so we needed to get this show on the road.

The judge grinned, handed the paperwork to his secretary, and escorted us to a grassy place beneath a big oak tree about 90 feet from his office door. Gina and I were dying with nerves, excitement, fear, and the thrill of our newfound calling to the world of espionage. We stood under the tree holding hands.

The judge got started with the ceremony, and just before he got to the part about "Frank, do you take Gina to be your lawfully wedded wife?" his secretary emerged from his office.

"Judge," she called, "may I speak with you for a moment?"

He was such a nice guy. "Excuse me," he called to her. "Now is not a good time. Could it just wait a few minutes, please?"

"No," she responded. "You need to take this call right now."

My heart was in my throat, but I played it cool. "You go ahead, Judge."

Well, our perfect plan had been foiled by the dear lady at the county office where we got the marriage license. I had left her window without taking the change from my $20 bill. I hadn't left any local phone numbers for her, so she grabbed a phone book and looked up our last names. She called the only Pignotti in the book, and sure enough, she'd gotten Gina's father on the phone.

Ring . . . ring.

"Hello?"

"Excuse me for calling," the nice lady said, "but is this the Pignotti residence?"

"Yes," said Dad.

"Do you have a daughter named Gina?"

"Yes," said Dad.

"Well," Nice Lady went on, "this morning when Gina was here to get her license, they left their change, and we have $12.50 for them. Would you like me to mail it to you, or will someone be coming by to pick it up?"

Bless her heart.

"What?" Dad said. "I don't understand. Gina already has a driver's license, and besides, she's at school."

"Oh, no, sir," Nice Lady chuckled. "It's not her driver's license; it's her marriage license."

Nuclear explosion.

"What the —?" Dad thundered. "Why didn't you stop them? She's only 16! Where is she now?"

Nice Lady wilted. "Well, Mr. Pignotti, they did ask about the nearest justice of the peace, and I recommended the county offices in Colton."

Dad hung up. By this time, Mom Pignotti was at his side, and when he filled her in, she went hysterical.

Dad's first call was to his good buddy Coy Estes, the chief of police in Upland.

"Coy," he rasped, "this is John. My daughter's run off with Frankie Pastore to get married. She's only 16. I think they might be in Colton with the justice of the peace."

"Well, John," said Chief Estes, "there's nothing I can do right now. No crime has been committed as far as I know, but I'll put out an unofficial APB for their car. What kind of car are they in?"

"They're in his dad's bronze 1963 Riviera."

"Good. That'll be easy to spot. Anything else? I'll call over to Colton right now to see if they're there. If they are, I'll have them detained till we get there."

In Colton, the nice judge excused himself and turned to walk back to his secretary. It was so quiet I could hear some of the phone conversation.

"Yes, they're right here," I heard.

A few seconds later, the judge came back out.

"Frank, Gina, I can't marry you because, Gina, you're underage. Honey, that was your father. He knows you're here, and there's an APB out on your car, Frank. Let's just sit down and talk about this. It's obvious you love each other very much, and if you're willing to go to all this trouble, I'm sure something can be worked out."

It was an obvious stall ploy. I had read it a hundred times in Ludlum's novels. The spy was trying to detain the target long enough for the sniper to get into position to take the shot. We had to get out of there. I had maybe 10 minutes before I had to make a move. If Dad was in the car, he was probably about 20 minutes away, going 90 miles per hour on Interstate 10.

I wasn't a fan of getting arrested, nor was I interested in a big car chase for the evening news. I began counting off the seconds in a corner of my racing mind, on full alert.

The judge escorted us back to his chambers and asked us to sit down. "Gina, tell me what's going on," he began.

With that, all of the emotion that had been building up inside her broke loose. She started to cry. "You don't know my father!" she sobbed. "He's got a terrible temper."

"Well, I'm going to need to talk with him," he said, "What's your number?"

"I don't think you'll be able to talk to him right now," Gina responded. "He's going to be really mad." But she gave him the number, and he dialed. Part of me was hoping he'd answer; at least that would reset the getaway clock back to zero.

"Hello, Mr. Pignotti," the judge said smoothly. "This is Judge Jones, and I have your beautiful daughter sitting in front of me."

We could hear Gina's dad screaming from where we sat.

"You listen to me," he yelled. "Don't let them out of your sight, because when I get that son of a b—, I'm going to break his legs, okay? You keep them right there. I know a lot of powerful people in this town, and if you know what's good for you, you'll do what I say."

Mr. Pignotti slammed the phone down. The judge hung up.

"Well, Gina," he said mildly, "you're certainly right about your dad. But you're safe here. Nothing will happen to you while you stay here. But right now, I have to get to court for a little bit. I'll be right back.

"And when I get back, I'm going to call a friend of mine who will understand the situation. She can help, and we'll meet with your parents in a public place to talk about this like adults, okay?"

I nodded to Gina to agree.

"Okay," she lied.

The judge got up and walked out. It was eerily quiet after Dad's tirade. We could hear the mechanism of the clock on the wall. What seemed like an eternity was probably about 15 seconds.

"Gina," I said, "we gotta go."

"I know," she sighed. "Let's get out of here."

On the judge's desk were our unstamped marriage certificate and our license. I picked them both up. We slowly opened the door and peered out to see if we could escape unnoticed. By now, there was a handful of people in the outer office.

I grabbed Gina's hand, and we hustled down the short hallway to the front door, hunching down to hide behind the counter as we made our hasty exit. Through the doors we bolted into a run for the Riviera.

We were now fugitives from the law.

15

★ ★ ★

BONNIE AND CLYDE

Because of the APB, we couldn't take any of the anticipated routes. So I-10 was out. And we knew they'd probably be expecting us to drive to Mexico or Vegas, so Interstate 15 was out. The best route to LAX would probably be the 60. I swung the old car in that direction, and when I approached my first California Highway Patrol officer, it dawned on me that it wasn't a great idea to have Gina in the passenger seat. It was 100 degrees, and the Riviera had no air-conditioning. The windows were down, the glass-pack mufflers were roaring along . . . and there was Gina, crouched on the floor of the car for the 90 minutes it took us to get to LAX.

By the time we arrived, our throats dry, our bodies soaked with sweat, and Gina's hair swirled into a thick mat, we were about half an hour behind schedule. But with no bags to check, we thought we might be able to make it in time. This was way before airport security existed, a fact that helped us immensely.

I parked the Riviera near where my dad had parked a week earlier when he picked me up from my flight from Nashville, and we ran to the Delta desk. It was 20 minutes before takeoff by the time we got to the front of the line.

With all my careful planning, I had missed a crucial point. Robert

Ludlum would have been disappointed. When I booked our flight, I had used an alias. The tickets were there for us, but when I whipped out my checkbook to pay for them, the names didn't match, and the ticket person wouldn't take the check.

I pleaded.

No use. She called for a supervisor. I had to think quickly.

"May I help you?" asked the supervisor.

"Yes, thank you," I said smoothly. "We'd like to buy our tickets."

"But sir," she responded. "Federal regulations require that you travel under your real name for purposes of identification should something unforeseen happen."

This never came up in Ludlum.

I took a long shot. "Yes, ma'am, I understand that. But, you see, I'm a pitcher with the Cincinnati Reds, we're in a tight pennant race with the Dodgers, and I've got an injury that we're trying to keep out of the press." I showed her my Cincinnati Reds ID card, driver's license, and splinted finger.

"Well," she said, impressed by my credentials and seduced by the idea of being part of the conspiracy, "yes, we can accept your check, but we'll have to change the manifest to reflect your real names, regardless. Is that okay? I'm sorry, there's nothing else I can do. Federal regulations."

It was the best I could do at the moment. At least there were three other flights with my name on them, and I doubted that Mr. Pignotti would trace them all.

"Yes, ma'am," I responded. "That would be fine."

"Frank Pastore and Gina Pignotti, then?" she asked.

"No," I said. "We're married, and we haven't had time to change her license. See?"

Gina held up her wedding band.

"All right," the supervisor said, handing us the tickets. "Here you go, but you'd better hurry. That flight is boarding right now, and the gate is all the way at the end of the concourse."

We thanked her and started running.

Gina was wearing high-heeled, wood-soled Candies, a popular shoe at the time. We sprinted down the long tiled corridor. *Click-click, click-click, click-click.* Gina sounded like a filly running through a mall.

Suddenly the rhythm changed. *Click-clop, click-clop, click-clop.*

Gina tugged on my arm to stop and ran back a few steps to retrieve the heel that had broken off. Then she just ripped off both shoes, and we kept running, running for the end of the concourse.

I could see the sign in the distance: "Birmingham." People were in line, boarding.

I put Gina in the line. "I've got to call my dad," I panted, "so he knows where his car is."

I ran to a bank of pay phones—no cell phones in 1978—found a dime, and dialed.

"Dad!" I said. "It's Frankie. No time to explain. I'm at LAX. The Riviera's parked near where you picked me up last week, and your keys are on the air cleaner under the hood. Gotta go, bye."

I never heard him say anything other than "Hello?"

I turned and ran to the gate. The doors were shut, and I could hear the jet engines roaring.

Oh my G—! I screamed inside. I pounded on the door and starting shaking the handle back and forth.

Instantly, attendants were all over me. "Sir! Sir! Can we help you?"

"Yes!" I screamed. "My wife's on that plane, and we're supposed to be together. Stop the plane!"

"Sir! Calm down. What flight are you on?"

"Birmingham!" I wept, pawing the door and watching the plane pull away from the gate.

"Sir!" the attendant shouted. "This is the flight to *Atlanta!* Birmingham is over there."

She pointed to the next gate, where no one was in line. They were getting ready to shut that door too.

Where was Gina? Was she going to Atlanta? Was she going to Birmingham? Did she get on the right flight? Which door should I choose?

Just then, the two attendants at the Birmingham gate turned to look down the Jetway. I ran toward them like a crazy man. As I got closer, waving my ticket, I could hear some kind of ruckus.

"Miss!" people were shouting. "We've got to close the doors. This is unacceptable! Take your seat and put your shoes on!"

"No! I can't!" I heard. "He's coming! He'll be here any second! I can't go without him! I know he's coming!"

It was Gina. Sprinting, I made the turn, and we saw each other in the Jetway. It was just like a slow-motion shampoo commercial: I ran toward her; she ran toward me, her long hair swirling behind her. We kissed. Time stood still. For us, at least.

By now the captain and the co-captain were out of the cockpit. A cluster of flustered flight attendants was at the door of the plane.

"Sorry about that," I said grandly.

We boarded the plane, which was of course full of seated passengers, who were by now intensely curious about what in the heck was going on.

So here we came—me, the guy with the sweaty, stringy hair matted to his brow, in a pastel disco shirt and jeans, and the cute young girl, barefoot with wild hair and mascara running down her cheeks, carrying her shoes and a wrinkled brown paper bag.

Our seats were, of course, in almost the last row. As we passed down the aisle, we might as well have had snakes growing out of our heads. Everyone stared, silently.

We arrived at our row. I squished into the window seat, second to the last row, and put Gina in the middle.

It was finally over, I thought. In a few minutes we'd take off. Things hadn't gone according to plan, but like any good spy, I could devise a backup plan. Let's see . . . we still had to get married. We'd arrive in Birmingham; I'd call my mom to come get us at the airport. It would be her turn to be shocked. Then in the morning we could take her car and drive up to Nashville to get two new Tennessee blood tests—unless they honored California's—pick up my stuff at my apartment, grab my new car, and drive back to California, where Gina's dad wouldn't be able to do anything, since our marriage would be a done deal.

The captain interrupted my thoughts.

"Ladies and gentlemen," he said, "we're sorry for our little delay, but now we're going to taxi out from the gate, and we'll be airborne shortly. Thank you for your patience."

I looked out the window as we backed away from the gate. It felt so good to see that concourse receding in the distance. Gina held my hand tightly.

What is she thinking? I thought. She's leaving everything to run away with me . . . everything. All she has are literally the clothes on her back and whatever the heck is in that brown bag.

Gina's makeup was smeared all over her face, her cute little heels were history, and her hair was a mess. She had never looked more beautiful.

Oh, G—, I moaned inside. *I love her so much.*

The PA crackled back on. "Ladies and gentlemen," said the captain, "we are now number two for takeoff. Please make sure all your tray tables are up, your seats are in the upright position, and your personal items are stowed securely under the seat in front of you. Flight attendants, prepare for takeoff."

A minute or two later the engines roared, and we started rolling down the runway.

Then I saw it. A dark blue, four-door Ford speeding across the tarmac, headed in our direction. The crescendo of sound and speed began to diminish. We were slowing down.

The darn pilot came back on. I was starting to hate him.

"Ladies and gentlemen, we have been called off the runway. There is nothing to be alarmed about. Please remain in your seats. This will be just a momentary interruption. Please remain calm."

They've got you! my mind screamed. *They just wanted to see if you would take off, because you haven't broken any serious laws yet, other than forgery. But now you've expressed the intent to transport a minor across state lines, and that's a felony. Your career's over, hot shot. You won't be with Gina either. You're going to prison.*

We didn't even return to a gate. The plane rolled to a stop on an unused runway. Men appeared from nowhere and wheeled a freestanding staircase up to the plane. They opened the door. The captain emerged from the cockpit and met two men in suits and dark sunglasses at the door. They reached into their breast pockets and flashed their badges.

The captain nodded. One presented a photograph to the captain and the two attendants. They stared at it a moment, then looked toward the back of the plane.

The rest of the passengers were putting two and two together. The earlier commotion caused by Disco Shirt Guy and Barefoot Mascara Girl was obviously connected with these federal agents and the fact that they had stopped a plane full of passengers right in the middle of takeoff.

I could see people looking at us. *Oh, G—! they were thinking. It's those kids. They're on the run from the law. Like Bonnie and Clyde. Get down, Mabel! I bet they've got a gun!*

One of the men, sunglasses still on, wearing his dark coat and tie when it was about 110 degrees outside, began a slow walk down the aisle like Tommy Lee Jones in *Men in Black*. He looked to the left, then the right, comparing each passenger with the photograph in his hand.

Step, look left, look right. Step, look left, look right.

As each row cleared, its passengers of course leaned forward in their seats and turned fully around to see just who the fugitives were.

Step, look left, look right. The guy was getting closer. And I knew *he* had a gun.

I had to bite the insides of my cheeks to keep from shouting out, "I'm here! I'm guilty! Leave the girl alone; she's got nothing to do with this!"

"Gina!" I whispered. "Get a magazine. Act like you're reading. Look normal!"

Right. As if normal in this situation was perusing the in-flight magazine, trying to decide between the luggage set and the Delta Airlines shot glasses.

The G-man was directly in front of us now. I looked down,

inspecting my knees, glancing sideways at Gina to notice that she was holding her magazine upside down.

He was at our row. I could peripherally see the girl on the aisle seat look up. Gina looked up. I looked up. The agent's face was expressionless.

Up until now, his cadence had been rhythmic, like a metronome, but now he lingered at our row. Yep, he was staring at me, for just a moment more than everyone else. But then he took another step.

There's only one more row, I thought. *What's he doing?*

Then I knew.

He thinks I'm packin' a gun, so he wants to get behind me, and the next thing I'm gonna feel is the cold, hard steel of a .38 against the base of my neck.

Frozen with fear, I looked up again. People had popped up in their seats like prairie dogs emerging from their holes. Every face in the entire plane was staring at me, their eyes accusatory. They knew.

But there was no cold steel at my neck. The agent checked the last row, the restrooms, the galley, and then walked briskly to the front of the plane. He and the other fed nodded to the captain, and then they were gone. The door was shut, the portable stairs were rolled away, and within five minutes we were airborne to Birmingham.

I knew what was going on. The judge had reported us, they had pulled Gina's photo from the DMV and faxed it over to the FBI or the DEA or whoever those guys with the dark suits and the sunglasses were, and they were just confirming that Gina was on board. When we landed in Birmingham, I'd be met by the authorities and get hauled off to jail.

The four-hour flight went far too fast. I was a guilty man jetting to my doom. Dead man flying.

It was almost dark by the time we landed. I wanted us to be the last two off the plane so as not to draw any further attention than necessary when the feds rushed in and slapped handcuffs on me.

The plane's aisle was a mile long. I knew the authorities would be in the Jetway. But they weren't. *That's because they're at the gate*, I thought. But they weren't there either.

Gina and I walked in a daze toward the baggage terminal and the airport exit. Every time I saw a badge, I'd almost start walking toward it to make the takedown easier.

Nobody stopped us. We got outside. Nobody stopped us there either. We still weren't married, but Bonnie and Clyde had made it to Birmingham.

16

★ ★ ★

WHAT HAPPENS WHEN FELONS SIGN YOUR MARRIAGE LICENSE

I went to a pay phone outside the airport to call my mom. At first she didn't believe me. Then she said it was too far for her to drive to the airport, too much trouble, and that we should take a cab to her house—a hundred-dollar fare that we didn't have.

I was ticked.

"Mom, you get your butt down here right now!" I shouted.

A while later she pulled up alone in the 1975 Riviera I had bought for her with my bonus money.

"Where's Dude?" I asked.

"We'll talk about that later," she said.

Gina and I were starving, so Mom took us to Shoney's. The reason I had come to Birmingham wasn't because of my grand affection for Mom or her long-lost love, Dude. It was because my mother had told me that she had bought a big house and put it in my name.

Since I'd been with the Reds, Mom had stolen about twenty thousand dollars from me. She had insisted that her signature be on my banking account so that if I ever needed money while I was off playing ball somewhere, she could get it for me. Since I was so young when I got started, I hadn't questioned that.

I'd finally found out about it when the friendly manager at Chino Valley Bank asked me about the large withdrawals my mother had been making. I had trusted her, so I hadn't even looked at my bank statements. But he'd noticed it, and in the nicest way possible, he'd wanted to clue me in.

I had confronted her about this, and she came up with some song and dance about my half sister, some trucking company she had invested in with two of her brothers, the need for a down payment on the new house in Birmingham, and so much other stuff that I couldn't see straight.

"It was all for you, Frankie!" she sighed. "I wanted you to have a nice house, a house for you and Gina."

Well, after our exquisite dinner at Shoney's, Mom took us to "my" house. We were exhausted. Mom gave Gina and me the master bedroom, and we settled in for our first-ever night together. And no, we did not consummate our elopement.

The next morning, as planned, Gina and I hopped into my mom's car to drive to Nashville. Our first stop was the ballpark to get my stuff. It was Friday, September 1, and the season had ended the day before.

Gina stayed in the car, and I walked into the Nashville Sounds front office like nothing had happened. As I walked back to General Manager Larry Schmittou's office, the secretaries all gawked at me, surprised looks on their faces.

I popped my head in at Larry's door. "Hi, Larry!" I called to him. "How ya doin'?"

He looked up, shocked.

"Frank!" he sputtered. "Everybody's looking for you! The Reds have been calling; they're pretty upset. What did you do? Where's the girl? She's only 16? What are you thinking? Is she okay?"

He paused for a breath.

"Everything's fine!" I lied. "She's right here. Wanna see?"

I waved to Gina through the glass, and we opened the door.

She responded with her best beauty-pageant wave through the passenger window, smiling big.

"Wow, Frank," Larry said. "I don't know what to say, but you'd better call the Reds. You're in big trouble."

I'll cross that bridge another day, I thought. *Right now I've got to get married.*

I went to the secretary and got my last paycheck, grabbed my stuff out of the clubhouse, and then Gina and I headed off to the apartment where I lived with three other guys. We chatted with my surprised roommates, and eventually headed to the Nashville courthouse. It was now about three o'clock on Friday afternoon.

The courthouse people told us that our out-of-state blood tests wouldn't work and that we'd have to wait three working days for them. We raced over to the hospital, but the office was already closed. We'd have to come back on Monday for them to draw the blood.

We pulled into my mom's place in Birmingham at about nine o'clock that night to learn that Gina's dad had called looking for us. Mom, ever the ready liar, claimed she had thrown him off the scent by saying we weren't there.

At about two o'clock Saturday morning, the phone rang. I could hear my mom talking to Dad Pignotti. "No, John, I haven't seen them. I wouldn't worry too much; they're good kids. No, I haven't heard from them . . . No, I haven't heard from the Reds either . . . Yeah, if I hear from them, I'll let you know. I'm sure they're okay."

There was a pause, and then I heard my mom say, "John, she's fine. Really. She looks great."

I knew we were busted. A moment later my mother came to the door and said, "Gina, it's your father. He knows you're here."

Gina got up and went to the phone, quietly ready for her doom. I went with her, rubbing her shoulder while she talked.

"Hi, Daddy," she said sheepishly.

"Is this what you want?" her father asked.

"Yes, Daddy," she said. "You know I love Frank with all my heart."

"Honey, you know we were going to give you a church wedding once you graduated," he said.

This was news to Gina.

"Well," he continued, "you've left us with no choice, so I guess you have our blessing. I wish you hadn't done it this way, but you're my daughter, and I love you no matter what."

Gina burst into tears, and so did I once she told me what her father had said.

So we were no longer Bonnie and Clyde, fugitives on the run from the feds and the wrath of Mr. Pignotti.

But we still weren't married.

A week later, since we had the time and I finally had my own wheels, we were free to take Gina shopping. The poor girl had worn the same clothes day after day and desperately needed everything. Especially a pair of shoes.

Mom had uncharacteristically invited some relatives over. They talked about how great it would be for us to be living in town near them in our own house, and I thought about how much had changed in just three days. I had an almost wife, I owned a house, I had a yard, and hopefully I'd have what was left of a baseball career—if the Reds would have me.

On Sunday I said that I needed to call my father. Mom said that she needed to talk to me first. Alone.

"No," I said. "Anything you say to me you can say to Gina, too."

She reluctantly complied. "Frankie, Dude and I aren't going to work out. I don't have enough money to live on my own, and you don't make enough to support me. So here's what we need to do. I need Daddy's pension. So you need to call your father. Tell him that you want him here with you and Gina, that you want us all to live here in your house. He won't listen to me, but he'll listen to you."

"But, Mom," I said, aghast, "you divorced him! I took him to get the papers notarized myself. He cried for weeks. But now he's happy living in Upland on his own."

"Frankie," my mother said flatly, "if you don't do it, you're going to lose your house, you won't have anywhere to live, and all the money you've got in it, all the equity, will be gone . . . all of it."

Somehow she still had her hooks in me, and I did something I've regretted ever since. I called my dad and lied to him. I deceived him—all because my mother, this pathological, manipulative, unfaithful sociopath, had found out that her lifelong lover didn't have the money she thought he had.

Dude was supposed to be her sugar daddy and take care of her. But he was still the con man he'd been when he and my mom were young, snazzy on the outside but a complete fake. Mom said Dude had preyed on women all his life, but my mom was playing the same game with him. They each thought they were going to live off the other.

But she had finally gotten onto him and kicked him out . . . and used me to lure my father back into her web after he had escaped and was building a decent life on his own. That call may have been the most evil thing I've ever done.

Dad agreed to drive from Upland to Birmingham and would arrive in a few days. As he was on his way, he got to the California-Arizona border Monday morning at about 10 o'clock. He was of course driving his own car that he had retrieved from LAX after I'd left it there on Elopement Day. But in all the excitement after Mr. Pignotti and Gina had reconciled, no one had thought to pull the APB on the bronze 1963 Buick Riviera, driven by one Frank Pastore.

So there's my dad, buzzing along, and a state trooper pulls him over. He gives the police officer his license, which of course read "Frank Pastore," which was his name as well.

The young trooper thought he'd hit the jackpot and nabbed the bad guy. No doubt he thought my dad was some old-man pervert who'd abducted a poor 16-year-old girl. He called my dad out of the car.

"Sir," he said, his hand on his weapon, "please exit the vehicle."

My dad got out amiably. He had nothing to hide.

Next thing he knew, the officer had whirled him around and pushed his nose into the bronze paint of his car.

"Get your hands on the car," he barked at my father. "Spread 'em!"

Then the guy called for backup. Another officer arrived and opened the trunk, no doubt expecting to find little Gina tied up with duct tape. Since she wasn't there, they assumed that my dad had disposed of her somewhere in the desert.

It took hours of phone calls to clear up the case of mistaken identity and the outdated APB. In the end, the officers finally let my dad go, and he continued on his less-than-merry way toward Birmingham.

Meanwhile, Gina and I went back to Nashville to get our blood drawn. The results would be back on Thursday. We were driving back to Birmingham in my car, which had just come back from being "repaired" at the shop, when it started thudding and smoking. We got in the slow lane and were babying it along to Birmingham.

Gina had dozed off, her head on my shoulder, when suddenly a huge sheet of glass flew off the truck in front of us, hung in the air for a moment, and then crashed down through our windshield, which shattered too. It sounded like a shotgun blast. Broken glass was everywhere.

I braked, and we made it to the shoulder. A guy came running up from the truck that had been behind us.

"Man, are you all right?" he yelled.

"I don't know," I said.

"I thought I'd find somebody dead," he gasped. "That was awful! You should be dead. God must be with you."

At that moment I didn't think much of it. But later in our life journey, I decided that truck driver was right. There would be many times through the years to come when we'd be cruising along just fine, and then *boom*, life as normal would be shattered. But God was with us, that day and every day since.

The safety glass of my windshield was in a million nubbled pieces. I drove to the gas station at the next exit with my head sticking out the driver's side window. The nearest auto-glass place was more than an hour away. There was nothing the kid at the Exxon station could do.

I grabbed a hammer to punch out a portal to look through, but that wouldn't work. So we just took out the whole windshield. The Exxon kid helped me, and I helped him clean up the broken glass that was all over his gas station. Gina and I got back on the freeway, our sunglasses giving us some protection against the glass fragments that swirled out of the windshield frame on the 90-minute trip back home.

Thursday came. We went to Nashville and were told there was a problem with our blood work. Come back tomorrow. We made our little three-hour jaunt back to Birmingham. We'd been gone eight days, and Gina was wondering if she would ever really get married.

Early Friday morning, we left again for Nashville. We picked up the blood work and headed over to the courthouse, where we were brought before a nice old Southern judge right out of Hollywood.

"Frank Pastore?" he drawled. "I've seen you pitch, son. Smokin! And who's this pretty little lady? You a Soundette, honey?"

Gina giggled. He'd thought she was one of the team's cheerleaders. "No, sir," she said softly.

"Well, well," he continued. "You sure you kids don't want to wait till after lunch? I'm awful hungry. I'm supposed to meet some friends for lunch, and I don't want to be late."

"*No, sir!*" we responded in chorus, as if we'd practiced.

"We don't need a long ceremony or anything," I said earnestly. "A quickie will do just fine."

"Well, okeydokey," His Honor replied. "A quickie it will be."

We walked into the courtroom. Two guys were sitting there, handcuffed, waiting for arraignment. They were being charged with the armed robbery of a liquor store the night before. They smelled as if they'd been sampling the merchandise before they'd attempted the holdup.

The judge walked us up before the bench. "We need, uh, two witnesses," he said, looking over the top of his glasses.

He kind of jerked his chin toward the two handcuffed guys, his eyebrows up.

At this point, I didn't care who witnessed this thing. I just wanted to be married. Gina shrugged.

"How about these guys?" I said.

Their names were Willie and Leroy. They were delighted to give us a hand, even though they were handcuffed and shackled. They hopped over next to us, their chains clanging on the floor, and looked gravely at the judge.

"All right," His Honor said.

It took about 90 seconds. "Frank," said the judge, "do you take Gina to be your wife?"

"I do!" I really meant it after all we'd been through.

"Gina, do you take Frank to be your husband?"

"I do," said Gina fervently.

"Does anyone have reason that these two should not be united?" asked the judge. "If so, let him speak now or forever hold his peace."

Willie and Leroy remained silent as mice as they signed the document.

"Awright," proclaimed the judge joyously. Lunch was coming soon. "Then by the power vested in me by the State of Tennessee, I do now pronounce you man and wife. Congratulations. You may kiss the bride."

I did, grateful beyond belief. Our new best friends, Willie and Leroy, nodded and clapped as best they could, their chains clanking like the sound of fans in the stands after a World Series shutout.

17

★ ★ ★

ANIMAL MAGNETISM

After the judge pronounced us man and wife, and Willie and Leroy shuffled away, we realized we were as starved as the judge. We crossed the street in front of the courthouse, found an Arby's, and devoured our wedding feast, a couple of roastbeef sandwiches.

From there it was back to Birmingham.

Dad arrived, and we fell into our "act normal in spite of everything being abnormal" roles. Only this time, Gina kept blowing her lines, asking me annoying questions, even respectfully confronting her new mother-in-law about things that didn't make sense.

So it was a relief when it was time to go off to Instructional League in Tampa. Gina and I gratefully hit the road—along with two ferrets we were babysitting for our friend Dave. Gina didn't have a strong love of ferrets, which she considered to be nothing more than skinny weasels, but we agreed.

On our long drive to Tampa, we let the ferrets, Elton and Bernie, run loose in the car. We didn't want them to get depressed by being cooped up in a cage. So we were tooling along the highway, Elton John songs blasting from the eight-track in honor of the weasels, when we suddenly realized that Elton had gone missing.

We pulled over, panicked. We looked under the seats, in the luggage, in the glove compartment, everywhere. We called, "Elton! Elton!" like crazy people. Bernie was beside himself, mourning for his lost partner.

Then we heard Elton scribbling and scratching somewhere in the vehicle, but the sound was muffled, almost as if he was on the engine block or something.

"Elll-tonnn!" I bellowed.

Then, peering into the air-conditioning vent above the radio, my wandering eyes beheld two beady little ferret eyes peering back at me.

"Elton!"

He had somehow crawled up into the dash, into the ducts, and worked his way up to the vent itself. But ferrets won't go into reverse on command. Elton was panicking a little, and so was I. He didn't know how to back himself out of his situation.

So, of course, I had to break open my car vent to get him out.

Gina and I arrived in Tampa. We moved into these really "affordable" apartments where I had lived before. I knew the owners, the Arena brothers: Andrew, Sammy, and Anthony. Andrew and his wife, Judy, had become my surrogate family over the years. The family matriarch, Grace, was the apartment manager. Grace was the prototypical Italian grandmother. She was short and plump, with curly gray hair, usually wearing an apron as she bustled about, making her iron will known in an energetic mixture of broken English and Italian.

Every day I would go off to practice, and Elton and Bernie would amuse themselves by attacking my child-bride, Gina. She couldn't stand living with the weasels. So she would shut them up in the broom closet until I got home. This didn't do much for their state of mind.

One fine day Grandma Grace came to visit Gina. The ferrets hadn't yet been stowed in their closet, and they were feeling frisky. Elton attacked Grace, biting her on the leg. Grace stomped around the tiny apartment, yelling in Italian and swinging her leg to disengage Elton, who was flying back and forth in the air, thinking this was the most fun he'd had in weeks.

Grace was cursing in Italian, yelling at the top of her lungs, "*Andare al diavolo!* Go to the devil! *Andare al diavolo!*" Gina was running after Grace with a broom, trying to shoo Elton away. Elton figured out that he was out of his league, so he let go, flew through the air, landed with a thud, and scurried away to hide under our bed.

"*You!*" Grace shouted at Gina, jabbing her finger in Gina's face. "You getta ridda that little son of a b—, or I'm-a gonna getta ridda you!"

With that she whirled around and stomped out the door.

Gina already believed that Elton was a demon, and that Bernie, the albino ferret, with his ghost-white fur and evil red eyes, was possessed. This episode sealed the deal. Fortunately our buddy Dave came back to town. The ferrets left, we exorcised the apartment, and all was well with Gina and Mama Grace.

Even though Gina and I were newlyweds stretching every dollar, we were out at the mall one night, and I somehow fell in love with the most expensive dog at the pet store. He was a saluki. I was told that the pharaohs of ancient Egypt used salukis as hunting hounds and that they were bred for speed, endurance, and leaping ability. I was warned that the dog would need a lot of room, a lot of exercise, and a lot of grooming, and to never let him off the leash in an unsecured area.

He cost me five hundred dollars, way too much money for us back

ONE PITCH FROM HUMILITY

DODGER STADIUM,
LOS ANGELES, JUNE 4, 1984

"You're always only one pitch away from humility," Johnny Bench told me on my first day in the big leagues. Five years later I made that pitch. I threw a 2-1 fastball to Steve Sax, which he hammered back at my face. I flinched. And the ball crashed into my right elbow—shattering my baseball dreams.

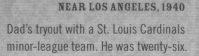

NEAR LOS ANGELES, 1940

Dad's tryout with a St. Louis Cardinals
minor-league team. He was twenty-six.

OSAKA, JAPAN, 1945

Dad was thirty-one.

THE MAIN CHARACTERS

⌄ UPLAND, CA, 1969

Eight-year-old Gina celebrated her
first Holy Communion in her backyard.

⌃ 1977

Gina and Papa at a
father-daughter dance.

★ ★ ★

1975

My high school graduation picture. Heavily airbrushed, thankfully.

1961

Elvis impersonator.

UPLAND, CA, SEPTEMBER 6, 1977

A rare photo of my parents together. Pictured here at Gina's parents' twenty-fifth wedding anniversary.

ONTARIO (CA) AIRPORT, JUNE 4, 1975

High school friends saw me off to Billings, Montana, to start my career with the Reds. I was seventeen. *From left:* Danny Monroe, Steve Schiro, me, Beverly Faucette, and Jorge Gomez.

★ ★ ★

SAN JOSE (CA) LITTLE LEAGUE, 1965

My first baseball picture. Note my teeth matched the team name.

˅ UPLAND (CA) AMERICAN LITTLE LEAGUE, 1970

I was twelve. Dad was the coach. I don't think he ever missed one of my games until I graduated from high school.

★ ★ ★

UPLAND COLT LEAGUE ALL STARS, 1973

The only baseball photo that has me with my two "dads."
Back row: far left, my father; *third from the left*, me;
far right, Gina's dad, John Pignotti. I was fifteen.

MY BASEBALL START

★ ★ ★

UPLAND (CA) MEMORIAL PARK, 1976

Dad in front of the bronze plaque the city embedded into the snack bar. For more than twenty years, he spent almost every day at that ballpark. (This is the photo I thought was lost.)

❯ HERSCHEL GREER STADIUM, NASHVILLE, 1978

I was the first Nashville Sound to make it to the Major Leagues.™

THROWING HARD AND FALLING IN LOVE

STADE MUNICIPAL, QUEBEC, 1977

I presented Mom and Dad with the game ball after a complete game—a one-hitter in a Reds AA game pitching for the Trois-Rivières Saints.

★ ★ ★

★ ★ ★

**OPENING DAY,
RIVERFRONT STADIUM,
CINCINNATI, OH, 1979**

Making the first pitch of
my Major League™ career.

**∧ RIVERFRONT STADIUM,
SEPTEMBER 28, 1979**

The Reds had just clinched the
National League West, after I tossed
my first Major League™ shutout.

RIVERFRONT STADIUM, AUGUST 23, 1982

Right after hitting my first Major League™ home
run—one that actually counted. I had my truly
first home run rained out on April 19, 1981.

★ ★ ★

IN THE BIG LEAGUES

**< SAN DIEGO,
CA, 1982**

Yucking it up with
the world-famous
San Diego Chicken
and our second
baseman, Ron
Oester. Ron's wife,
Jackie, and Gina
were close friends.

★ ★ ★

^ WEST COVINA, CA,
MAY 31, 1981

Frankie at the Queen
of the Valley Medical
Center's neonatal facility.

⌄ RIVERFRONT STADIUM, 1983

Frankie with catcher Johnny Bench.

ADDING TO TEAM PASTORE

^ GRANDMA PASTORE'S
DRIVEWAY IN EAGLE
ROCK, CA, 1961

Dad was always behind me,
lifting me up and encouraging
me to go "higher" in life than
he ever did. I have, but only
because he first provided
the ladder that made it
all possible—the ladder
of baseball.

^ REDSLAND, TAMPA, FL, MARCH 1983

A father should strive to make his son into a better
man than himself. I've succeeded.

★ ★ ★

CLAREMONT, CA, JUNE 12, 2003

My princess graduates from Claremont High School.

FEBRUARY 1985

Christina and me. I think every dad should get to shampoo his daughter's hair once a year . . . just because. Today she's a hairstylist, thanks to me.

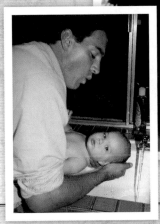

SCOTTSDALE, AZ, OCTOBER 29, 2005

At my niece Tenlee Pignotti's wedding to Brian Vroom. *From left:* my son, Dr. Frank Pastore; his wife, Jessica; my daughter, Christina; my bride, Gina; and me.

★ ★ ★

BIOLA UNIVERSITY, LA MIRANDA, CA, 1995

Me as a professor.

‹ SAN DIMAS, CA, JANUARY 25, 2007

A "road trip"—on location at a local church.

FROM BASEBALL . . .

EL SALVADOR, AUGUST 25, 2005

I had the privilege of meeting Franklin, the child we sponsor through World Vision.

★ ★ ★

LOS ANGELES, DECEMBER 2003

Glna came wlth me for our show's first publicity shots. She's my life's co-host, and the Lord is our Executive Producer.

TO BROADCASTING

Photo by Harry Langdon, Jr.

< HYATT REGENCY, IRVINE, CA, APRIL 2005

Proof that I have, in fact, for special occasions, worn something other than jeans, boots, and black T-shirts.

★ ★ ★

> NOVEMBER 2005

Ann and John Pignotti
(Gina's mom and dad).
This was taken one
year before his death.
They were married for
fifty-four years.

< DODGER STADIUM,
LOS ANGELES, 2008

Me with the greatest sportscaster
of all time—Vin Scully.

FUN, FAST, AND REAL

BETWEEN
REVELSTOKE AND
BANFF, CANADA,
2007

Livin' the dream!
And, in case you're
curious, the bike
has 109,000 miles
on her, and no,
she's not for sale—
neither is Gina.

★ ★ ★

˅ SOMEWHERE ON THE OREGON COAST, 2007

For my fiftieth birthday, five couples took a little bike trip—4,300 miles in eleven days—taking in Lake Tahoe; the Oregon and Washington coasts; Victoria, Whistler, Banff, and Lake Louise in Canada; Montana; Idaho; the deserts of eastern Oregon; Reno; and then back home to Los Angeles. I'd do it again tomorrow if I could. *Back row, from left:* Mark and Cindy Stapleton; Sean McDougal (his wife, Linda, is taking the picture); Bruce Erickson. *Middle row, from left:* Gina; me; Mimi and Dave Pentz. *Front row, center:* Teresa Erickson.

˅ UPLAND, CA, DECEMBER 2009

Our most recent Christmas picture. *From left:* Christina's boyfriend, Josh Smallwood; Christina; Gina; Michael; me; Frankie; Jessica; and our granddog, Cannoli.

★ ★ ★

A PRAYER FOR MICHAEL JOHN PASTORE

JUNE 11, 2009
Dear Lord, may this precious one
grow to become a man who seeks
after You above all earthly things.
Who, because he knows You,
trusts You, and because he trusts You,
loves You with all of his heart.
And grant me the days to swell that heart
with the fullness of this grandfather's love.

* * *

then. I named him Suki. Suki the saluki was a gorgeous animal. I loved him, and Gina loved him too, if only for the fact that he wasn't a ferret.

After Instructional League was over, we needed to drive back to LA. We decided to stop off in Birmingham to ask my mother to take care of Suki. I don't know why I thought that my mother would care for the dog any better than she had cared for me, but I guess I indulged in some sort of fanciful thinking. Mom promised to abide by the strict instructions I gave her, so I left this elite animal in her care. We'd be back in three months.

We returned to find that Suki had become a wild coyote. Unbathed since I left, he had a wound on his belly that had abscessed. He was full of ticks and needed medical treatment. He had lived outside the entire time, and Mom had occasionally thrown left-over food into a bowl on the porch for him to eat.

I was so furious that I cried. Here I was, this six-foot-two-inch professional baseball player, a grown man, weeping over this dog and howling at my mother that she had neglected him just as she had emotionally neglected me for years. What was wrong with this woman? Why had I been so stupid to entrust this dog that I loved to her "care"? She was incapable of caring for anything or anyone except herself.

We drove from Birmingham to Tampa, straight through, with Suki on a blanket in the backseat. We pulled into the Arena family's driveway. I took Suki out of the car and tied his leash to the hose bib next to some food and a bowl of water, and Gina and I walked into the house. We were going to greet the Arenas and then get Suki to the vet.

Within 30 seconds, I looked out the window and saw Suki racing up the street, sprinting like a greyhound. I ran outside, saw the gnawed-off leather leash, jumped into the car, and took off after Suki as fast as I could follow.

But Suki was gone.

Fortunately I didn't have much time to brood over this loss and all that it represented in my resentment toward my mother. The new baseball season was upon us, I had Gina by my side, and I was about to have what *Sports Illustrated* would call, for that year, "the best spring training in baseball."

18

★ ★ ★

ONE PITCH FROM HUMILITY?

In spite of my messed-up childhood, I'd grown up with normal all-American dreams. As a boy I pretended I was Tom Seaver pitching to Johnny Bench. Gina had grown up with her brother Johnny, the all-star catcher, pretending he was Johnny Bench.

So you can imagine how it felt for little Gina Pignotti Pastore to find herself at spring training, 1979, with, yes, the real Johnny Bench. And the real Tom Seaver. This was the Cincinnati Reds in their heyday, the Big Red Machine in all its baseball glory.

And we were part of it.

We were still an object of curiosity because of our Bonnie-and-Clyde elopement saga; Gina was getting the once-over and a lot of good-natured kidding. She was 17, and I was a mature 21 years old. The press loved our story: We were young, in love, attractive, talented . . . To them we embodied the American dream. Whatever that is.

That spring I was hoping to make the AAA team. I'd been the third-best starting pitcher in Nashville and was only hoping for a simple one-level promotion. On the first day, during the first hour of camp, all eyes were on three bull-pen mounds, where pitchers would throw to catchers. Tom Seaver was on one mound. Freddie Norman was on another. And yes, within about five minutes of arriving, minor leaguer Frank Pastore broke protocol and jumped up on that third mound, right in front of all the other big leaguers. Dozens of photographers and journalists were there; they loved it.

Tom was in the middle; Johnny Bench was catching him. Then Johnny got up, went over to my catcher, and tapped him to trade places. I was pitching to Johnny Bench for the first time in my life.

He called a fastball in. He didn't move his glove; I hit it. He called a fastball away. I hit it. He called a few more pitches. I nailed 'em. Johnny stood up and pushed up his face mask. He called the Reds' manager over. I was still on the mound and had no idea what they were saying. (Later I heard that Bench told the manager, "This kid's arm's ready. I don't know where his head's at, but this kid's got it.")

I did have it. Guys all around me were getting cut, and I was expecting to go down any second. Time went by. Then there were only about 12 pitchers left, and all the press people started saying I was going to the big leagues. Whenever they interviewed me, I hung my head and said how happy I was just to be there at all.

Even though I played it cool and joshed with reporters, I was in agony. I didn't know if I'd go back in the AAA minors in Indianapolis or somehow end up in Cincinnati with the Reds. Gina's dad arrived to drive her and our stuff to one of those two cities, and I flew to Cincinnati with the team. There were 11 pitchers. One still needed to be cut. I sure didn't want it to be me.

The next morning was opening day of the baseball season. I walked from the hotel to the ballpark. All I could think as I plodded along was "I'm gonna get cut. I'm gonna get cut."

I was one of the first guys to arrive. Bernie Stowe, the clubhouse manager, welcomed me as I walked into my very first Major League™

clubhouse. After all the raunchy, cockroachy locker rooms of the minor leagues, it was incredible. All the brand-new uniforms were hanging up, everything perfectly in place, every pair of cleats black and clean. I saw the various uniforms hanging on the outside of the lockers. I didn't see my name. I did see the name of my chief rival. He'd made it. Obviously I had not.

I turned, crushed. "But I'll come back," I told myself. "I can do this."

I leaned against a doorjamb, trying to get control of myself, and Bernie Stowe came around the corner.

"I didn't make it, did I?" I said to him.

"Oh, kid!" he said. "I got your uniform right here." He held up a pristine shirt with the number 35 emblazoned across the back.

I was speechless. "But . . . my number's 53," I mumbled.

"Oh," said Bernie. "Fifty-three's a minor-league number. You're in the majors now!"

I put that new uniform on. And there I was, Riverfront Stadium on Opening Day 1979, before a sellout crowd of 50,000. The national press was all there, and we were playing the San Francisco Giants. Tom Seaver started the game. I was on the bench.

Tom got into trouble early and had to come out of the game. By the fifth inning, we were losing 11-5 and had already used four pitchers. John McNamara, the manager, hollered down the bench.

"Kid, get up!"

As soon as I walked out of the dugout, the crowd erupted in cheers. I made my way to the bull pen and began warming up. Then I walked out to the mound. The scoreboard was ablaze with my name and my thus-far claim to fame: "Youngest Player in the National League." The crowd's standing ovation rang in my ears.

Johnny Bench gave me a wink, and away we went. I struck out the first player. The crowd was going crazy.

I pitched for three innings and gave up only one hit.

The Reds ended up losing 11-5, but you wouldn't have known it if you'd been watching me. After the game, photographers were all over me; fans were clapping and giving me the thumbs-up. I was having a great time, laughing with reporters, coming up with snappy one-liners. I was so green and stupid that I didn't know that even if you'd had an amazing game personally, if your team lost the game, you did *not* grant interviews. Period.

I ambled into the clubhouse. The other players were all there, of course, since they weren't idiots and hadn't been hanging out with the media. Johnny Bench motioned to me. I went over to his locker.

"Let's clear this up right now," he said. "There're two things you need to know about playing in the majors. First, it's a lot harder to stay here than it is to get here. And second, don't ever get too cocky or too arrogant, because you're always only one pitch away from humility."

Boom!

Much later I'd discover that he was absolutely right. But back then his advice was just one of those things you hear from older people. It may well be true, but it doesn't apply to you. Sitting on top of my world at age 21, I didn't want reality breaking into my fantasy. I didn't want to think about injuries, slumps, or losing streaks. I knew those things were possibilities, but I didn't want them to cloud my dreams.

All I wanted was success: a long, unbroken career of Major League™ pitching that would make me rich and famous. I wasn't on some quest for meaning and fulfillment; I knew exactly what would make me happy. A four-letter word: *more*. I just needed more money, more success, and more fame, and to achieve that, all I needed was more time.

After all, I believed that *I* had made myself into a Major League™ pitcher. I'd worked hard. I was good. I was a winner. Humility was for losers. On that first day in the bigs, I knew I was one of the best pitchers in baseball. The only small problem was that the rest of the league just didn't know it yet.

But they would know soon enough. I could still hear the roars of the crowd and the feel on the mound as I'd ripped those pitches over the plate. I appreciated Johnny Bench; after all, the man was a legend. But really, I didn't believe I was just one pitch from humility. I was one pitch from success.

19

★ ★ ★

OTHER THINGS I LEARNED FROM JOHNNY BENCH

Over the next five seasons, I set out for more and more. Along the way I would accumulate the trappings of a successful, young professional ballplayer. I would buy all the right status symbols. Gina and I would have the Porsche, the Mercedes, the house, the condo, and the clothes. I would even earn the respect of my peers, becoming the Reds' player rep. I would put money away in savings, start an off-season construction business, and have two great kids and a solid marriage. Down the line, in the years to come, I would live my dream. But it still wouldn't be enough. It was as if no matter how much I had, I was always hungry for more.

As I got started in my Major League™ career in the spring of 1979, Johnny Bench fortunately didn't hold my lack of humility against me. Actually, he kept his eye out for me and became a mentor and a friend. I'd idolized him since I was eight years old, and now here I was, in that big, clean, freshly painted Reds' clubhouse every day, watching Bench, Seaver, and my other heroes hang out. I was by far the youngest player on the team; the other guys all called me "kid."

One spring day I was at my locker when I overheard Bench and Seaver talking about a couple of books. I loved books. I turned, and there was Seaver handing Bench Dostoyevsky's *The Brothers Kara-mazov*. Bench was returning some book on advanced bridge to Seaver.

I walked over, magnetized.

"Ever read Dostoyevsky?" Bench asked me.

"No," I said. All I read were Robert Ludlum novels so I could plot my next great escape with Gina.

"You gotta read this," said Seaver. "It's a classic."

Bench followed up. "You know how to play bridge?"

I shook my head. Bridge was for old ladies . . . and, evidently, Major League™ legends.

"Then learn," Bench said. He tossed me a book on beginning bridge from off his locker shelf. "Read this and be ready to play on the next road trip."

Seaver nodded. It was like getting orders from the Pentagon.

The next day at the ballpark, while we were running our sprints in the outfield during batting practice, Seaver yelled at me. "Hey, kid! What's the point count for an opening one no-trump bid?"

I knew if I blew it, they'd give up on me, but if I passed, I'd be in. I thought for a moment.

"Is the point count 16 to 18 with even distribution?"

He smiled. "Yep. Nice job!"

I breathed a sigh of relief.

"Now, what's Blackwood?" he continued.

I had no idea. "I'm not there yet," I stalled.

"Keep reading," said Seaver, "and know it by Thursday."

Thursday was the getaway day for our next road trip. I was more nervous sitting down to play bridge with Tom Seaver, Johnny Bench, and Tommy Hume than I was pitching to any big-league hitter.

I lost a lot of money learning how to play bridge with those guys.

They taught me that setting up a hitter is like playing bridge. You've got to know your strengths, their weaknesses, and when to slough—and always to be thinking about your next play or pitch. Priceless.

Bench and Seaver also got me started on crossword puzzles.

"Hey, kid," Seaver called out to me from his locker one day. "I'm stuck. What's a three-letter word for 'obese'?"

Bench and a few of the other guys looked up, grinning.

Ever the anxious performer, I was ready to let them know how smart I was.

"F-A-T, fat!" I shouted proudly.

They howled, absolutely apoplectic that I had taken him seriously. I wanted to climb into my locker and die.

Once I came out of my locker a few weeks later, I began to enjoy some of the clubhouse visitors who'd stop by. In Los Angeles, comedians Tim Conway and Harvey Korman came to see us. Later we swore that Tommy Lasorda had sent them to exhaust us before the game—they did improv for about 20 minutes, and we all were laughing so hard, we couldn't get off the floor.

Another time, Don Rickles came in to give us a pep talk; it was really more of a roast of Johnny Bench and Tom Seaver. Great coaches would stop by as well—Bobby Knight, Bobby Bowden, Bear Bryant, as well as NFL coaches, Hollywood stars, and miscellaneous rich people. After all, this was the Big Red Machine, and our Hall of Famers were quite a draw. As I watched them in action, it was sweet to see the perks of fame. It was like a fraternity where, once you were in, you were automatically tight with everyone else who was famous, whether you knew them or not.

But if anybody showed me how to use the benefits of fame for something that really mattered, it was Johnny Bench. In Philadelphia once, we were getting on the team bus after a game. There were about 100 fans behind the security barrier, and a few armed guards were on hand to protect us from them. We loaded up and were rolling out when suddenly Bench yelled, "Stop the bus!"

He jumped out and ran toward the now-screaming fans, straight toward a little boy who couldn't have been more than six, sitting on his daddy's shoulders. Bench grabbed the Reds hat off the boy's head, signed it, scruffled his hair, put the hat back on his head, and then turned and jogged back to the bus.

The boy's eyes were huge, his mouth in the biggest smile I'd ever seen. The father had tears of gratitude in his eyes.

It was magic. *Wow!* I thought. *If only I could make some kid that happy one day.*

20

★ ★ ★

GETTING LOOSE

Around this time was also the beginning of what is taken for granted now: Female reporters were allowed in the locker room for the first time. Some of the guys seemed to get their thrills by parading around naked, but the women handled it professionally. Once we all got used to it, it soon became no big deal. You just got in the habit of putting a towel around you on the way from the shower to your locker. Those reporters sure did see a lot of bare butts, though.

Out in the bull pen during games, we'd look for ways to entertain ourselves. We'd have some of our best card games in the three bull pens of the National League where the fans couldn't see us: Shea Stadium in New York, Veterans Stadium in Philadelphia, and Dodger Stadium. But in the exposed bull pens in the other cities, there was nowhere to hide. So we'd have to be a little sneakier. You could usually get away with a crossword on a clip chart if you did it right, but more often than not, the bull-pen coach would frown on that kind of thing, and you'd be left looking for other distractions. Binoculars were fun, especially for watching things not on the field, like fights, strange-looking people, and girls working on their tans.

One of the great gags was to find a way to call the opposing bull pen and act as if you were the manager giving the order for someone to go warm up. He'd get up, and the next thing you know, a ticked-off manager on the other team would be calling down to their bull pen wanting to know why so-and-so was warming up. Great fun.

The worst thing that ever happened to me in the bull pen? We were at Fenway Park, I was getting loose in order to pitch, and a drunken fan was screaming down at me from the stands that are right above the mounds. I gave him some advice, and he threw what I thought was beer all over me. Then I smelled it. It was no longer beer, but no doubt it had once been beer. Gotta love those Red Sox fans.

During the off-season, I got invited to lots of charity golf tournaments. After my rookie year in 1979, Tommy Lasorda was the featured dinner speaker at one of them. There were lots of Dodgers players there, and a few of us from other organizations, just to fill out the roster.

Tommy thanked everybody for coming out to support the charity and asked his players to stand up and be recognized. He introduced each Dodger player and then said something like this: "And ladies and gentlemen, there's also someone very special here tonight. Someone who has done more to extend the careers of these great Dodger ballplayers than even me. On the days we knew this guy was going to pitch against us, I never had a player get sick or ask for a day off. Everybody wanted to hit off him.

"Frank Pastore of the Cincinnati Reds, are you here? There you are, please stand up."

The crowd howled.

I owed this great moment of ignominy to my first appearance in Dodger Stadium on May 25, 1979. It was easily the worst outing of my career. I had 30 people on the pass list, all my friends were there, and it was televised locally. It was my first appearance at home: the perfect time to do well.

Sadly, the Dodgers didn't cooperate. Seaver started but got into trouble early. Then Hume came in to get us out of the third, and I was brought in to start in the fourth with the score 7-2.

I had a rough inning; I gave up five runs on three home runs, making the score 12-2. I had one-two-three outs in the fifth but had more problems in the sixth. I gave up a leadoff home run, making the score 13-2; then after a walk, a strikeout, and a couple of infield singles, I had two guys on with one out when I faced Davey Lopes.

With the count three balls and no strikes, I threw a fastball down the middle, and Lopes hit a three-run homer, making the score 17-2 in the sixth. Mercifully, John McNamara—or "Mac" as we called our manager—got me off the hill. I had given up 10 earned runs on nine hits and a walk, including five home runs, in just $2^{1}/_{3}$ innings. I couldn't get a breaking ball over for a strike, and the Dodgers were just sitting on my fastball.

Five days later I threw a third of an inning in Houston and was sent down to the minors right after the game. I had thrown 25 innings in the big leagues and had an ERA (earned run average) of 7.48. Not good.

I vowed to return a "pitcher" instead of a "thrower" and took Mac's advice to improve my off-speed stuff. In the AAA, I went 7-2, and Mac called me back up after spending just 60 days in the minors. I ended the season throwing back-to-back shutouts, the first against Houston to maintain our half-game lead in the National League West, and the second to clinch at least a tie for the division title against Atlanta.

I started the second game of the play-offs against the Pittsburgh

Pirates and did well, but we lost in extra innings. The Pirates went on to win the World Series in seven games over the Baltimore Orioles. That entire off-season I had to watch myself giving up those five home runs on the Dodger highlight reel every time their commercial came on the cable channel.

The humiliation motivated me, though. I led the team in wins in 1980. Mac told me, after I had established myself as a legitimate big-league pitcher, that he wasn't sure if he'd ever see me back in the big leagues after the beating I took that night in Dodger Stadium. Many players never return from a public failure like that. I was fortunate to come back . . . and I was also fortunate I didn't get stuck in the mire of the seamy side of baseball.

21

★ ★ ★

REDS, GREENS, AND LIFE IN THE FASTBALL LANE

Baseball, like all pro sports, has its dark side, and it attracts a lot of underworld characters. I first learned this through a family friend I'll call Uncle Tony.

Uncle Tony was a colorful character from Chicago. In 1980 he invited some of his friends to come watch me play the first game of a three-game series against the Cubs at Wrigley Field. I borrowed some free game passes and put about eight people on the pass list. Their names all sounded ethnically Italian, and they were no doubt associates of Uncle Tony's.

That first day went by without a problem. When I got to the park the second game, John McNamara called me into the office. In there were two agents in dark suits, and they wanted to know my relationship with the people I had put on the pass list the day before. They said the names had been flagged by "the authorities," and they wanted to know how I knew them.

I told them that Uncle Tony had asked for some extra tickets for some friends. The agents asked me if I knew any of the other guys; I didn't. It turns out that Uncle Tony worked for a big labor union in Chicago, and the feds were keeping an eye on him and his "associates."

Cue *The Godfather* theme. I told Uncle Tony about it, and he just laughed. "Yeah, those guys have a tail on me wherever I go. They got a wiretap on the house too. No big deal, just part of the job, Frankie."

The authorities were always looking for the connections between organized crime, pro sports, drugs, you name it.

When I was in the minor leagues, the big drug was pot. The guys who did it regularly claimed they didn't get the hangover you get from alcohol. I had gotten high a few times in high school, but I was always so paranoid of getting caught that it wasn't much fun for me or whomever I was with. So, when the guys on the team would ask me to get high, I'd just politely decline. My preferred relaxant was Scotch, anyway.

To me, the drug thing just wasn't worth the risk. You could often tell who lit up by the telltale towel at the base of the door when you walked into their hotel rooms. Or the constant breath mints. You could always count on those guys for a Certs.

When I got to the big leagues, there were a lot of rumors about cocaine, but I never saw it in person. During my time, amphetamines were pretty common. They were known as "greenies," because of their light green color, and downing them was equivalent to drinking about 20 cups of coffee without the acid taste.

Most of the guys I knew who would "bean up" were those who had started their careers back when it was legal to take amphetamines, or those from foreign countries where it was still accepted, albeit illegal. They had become psychologically addicted to the drug and believed they couldn't play well without it.

Today it's still an issue. Prior to it becoming a prescription-only drug, the most common delivery form was in what was called "red juice." You'd stir up a thermos of red Kool-Aid with the amphetamine, and the veterans said if you drank a small Dixie cup of that stuff, in about 20 minutes you'd be revved up and rarin' to go. To help you come down, you could drink about a quart of milk right after the game.

Sometimes the greenie was mixed directly into a pot of coffee, giving a third option beyond unleaded and leaded: supreme. People told me you always had to make sure you got the pots right, or you could be awake for hours.

However, taking amphetamines was usually good only for hitters. If a pitcher juiced up, he'd get reckless. He'd think he was throwing harder than he really was, and he'd want to challenge everybody with his fastball. He'd no longer want to trick hitters with breaking stuff. He'd just want to throw harder and harder and harder, his judgment would get messed up, and he'd be less effective. Plus, it would make him vulnerable to injury, since he couldn't properly interpret the feedback his body was sending him regarding his elbow or shoulder.

While I was playing, I never knew anyone who—for sure—was taking steroids. But there were suspects. The usual profile went something like this: You'd see a guy who was a pretty good hitter, who hit lots of doubles in the gap with a few home runs. Then he'd show up at spring training after five months off, having gained about 30 pounds of pure muscle. His shoulders would be broader, his neck muscles more defined, his deltoids like grapefruit, his biceps like oranges, cut triceps, bulging forearms, and much bigger pecs. His quads and hamstrings would be chiseled underneath his uniform.

You'd ask, "What's up with so and so?"

And the answer you'd always hear would be, "He's been eating right, taking lots of protein supplements, and lifting lots of free weights."

Right.

Meanwhile, the guy's doubles in the gap were now flying out of the park, his homers were another 50 feet farther, his inside bat speed was a lot quicker, and bottom line, he was a tougher out. I'm glad baseball is coming down hard on guys who take banned substances. It puts the whole game under suspicion.

Another seamy area was, of course, the women. Constant women. Healthy young men with money to burn and a little fame makes for an alluring mix. If they're on the prowl, they'll score. What's funny is that so many guys think it's their smooth moves that make them so lucky in terms of getting women. The fact is, most of the time, they're the prey.

One year, at the beginning of the season, I got called into the manager's office to be introduced to three guys in suits. Protocol required that I, as the union player rep, be notified beforehand of any outsiders requesting access to the players. They briefly told me who they were and why they were there.

I agreed to let them in, and I called the guys together.

The talk went something like this: "Gentlemen, we're with the Drug Enforcement Agency, and we're here to warn you of the latest attempt by organized crime to infiltrate Major League Baseball.™ They will be trying to get to you in the following manner: Suppose you walk into your hotel lobby after the game and see a beautiful girl. You approach her and she agrees to accompany you back to your room. You get there, and she tells you she's unwilling to have sex with you unless you can get her some cocaine.

"Now, you may not have any, but you know who does. She's beautiful, you're revved up, so you go and score for her. While you're gone, she sets up the camera she has hiding in her purse and points it to the bed, or she lets in her accomplice, who hides in the closet with the camera.

"You return. She does a few lines, maybe with you, and then you hop in the sack. Once the incriminating pictures are taken, she, or her accomplice, breaks out a gun, shows you the camera, and tells you that unless you do what they tell you, your wife will see the pictures. They are targeting married players. They know every one of you. You'll be blackmailed to throw the game—a strikeout here, an error there, a couple fat pitches with the game on the line—anything you can do. We don't want that to happen. Consider yourselves forewarned, so be careful out there."

After that speech, we all turned paranoid. Every time we saw a pretty girl, we just knew she was working for the Mob.

"Look!" we'd whisper in hotel lobbies. "There's another one right over there!"

Thanks to the Mafia, there were a few formerly straying husbands who became newly faithful that year.

22

★ ★ ★

FORCED TO HANG WITH THE CHRISTIANS

Gina had already laid down the law for me regarding sex on road trips. We'd been married for only seven months by the time we broke camp in April 1979. Gina had already heard from the other wives that "things" happen on road trips, and she didn't want her new husband to be off philandering with the wild guys. She asked around and found out which players had good reputations and which ones didn't.

On the morning of our first road trip to Atlanta, on the way to the airport, I looked over at Gina in the passenger seat. She had a pen in her hand and was marking up a team roster.

"No . . . no . . . okay . . . maybe . . . definitely no, yes, yes, no, no," she was saying aloud as she either circled or put a line through various players' names.

"Baby, what are you doing?" I asked innocently.

"Oh, I'm letting you know who you can hang out with," she said.

"Oh, really?"

"Yeah," she said, handing me the list. "Here's who you can hang out with, and if I hear you're with any of these other guys, then I won't be here when you get back. I'll be at my parents' house."

She wasn't shrill or threatening; she was just stating a fact.

I resigned myself to the fact that I'd be hanging out with the "yeses." It wouldn't do any good to deny the simple reality we both knew. Beautiful women, Mafia hired or not, constantly hit on pro athletes, and a lot of ballplayers cheated on their wives.

I'm sure the pressure in pro ball is even worse these days. But even back then I got pressured to be unfaithful to Gina from the second I got married . . . and of course, once I said no, some of my teammates pressured me all the more, just for the fun of seeing me fall. Sometimes the forbidden fruit looked sweet, but I never tasted it, not on religious or moral grounds, but for a very practical reason. I loved Gina and didn't want to risk losing her. If I cheated on her, she would find out—wives always do—and she would leave me. If I wanted Gina, I had to stay true.

Early on, when one of the veteran players was asking me why I didn't fool around, I responded off the top of my head. "Why would I get excited about driving some used car," I asked him, "when I've got a brand-new Porsche waiting for me at home?"

The analogy stuck; years later at some formal event in Cincinnati, Johnny Bench came up to Gina and said, "You sure must be something special, because your husband doesn't mess around on road trips."

So, courtesy of Gina, I was now forced to hang out with the "goody-good" players on road trips. The Christians. That's not to say all the non-Christian guys fooled around, smoked pot, or did cocaine. They didn't. But the guys on Gina's list were the ones who stayed faithful, and everybody knew it. Especially the team wives. It wasn't that big of a deal, really, because the Christians were great guys. They may not have been the household names, but they were the most well-liked guys on the team. They didn't seem to have the giant egos and all the external flash of the other guys, and they had stability and maturity that I knew I lacked.

I tended to get too emotionally high after a good game and too low after a bad game, but these guys had an emotionally even keel that helped them endure the ups and downs of a long season. And most of all, they seemed to have a "real life" outside their baseball careers.

So the Christians were good guys. But I hated their annoying habit of cornering people after a bad game. I had a lot of bad games in my career, so I had to endure a lot of cornering. I'd be sitting on a bus or a plane, usually reading a book, bummed out over my poor performance, and sure enough, one of them would find his way over to me to strike up a conversation that always ended up on the topic of Christianity. They called it "sharing."

Fortunately I knew how to handle religious fanatics. It was a technique I had learned back in Catholic high school in California. It was my sophomore year, 1973, and after Mass one day outside the gym, a couple of seniors cornered me. They had just gotten "saved." It was at the height of the Jesus movement of the '70s. *Jesus Christ Superstar* and *Godspell* were big, and Jesus was newly popular since He had long hair and was a countercultural kinda guy.

All over California, hippies were coming to Jesus in droves. They were getting baptized, singing worship songs, toting their guitars everywhere, and starting churches. At our school, though, the "Jesus freaks" were the long-haired, bead-wearing, long-sideburned losers who didn't play sports, date girls, or drive cool cars. They were geeks from the audiovisual club—you know, the kind of guys many of us work for today.

Anyway, in high school I was cornered one day by a couple of Jesus freaks who started hammering me with this "Christianity isn't a religion; it's a personal relationship with Jesus" stuff. They asked me offensive questions like "If you died tonight, where would you go?" They even broke out an orange *Four Spiritual Laws* booklet and then, to my alarm, started going through it with me. I realized I had to do something to get them to stop.

So I started asking them questions: "If everything has a cause, what caused God? If your God is so good and powerful, why is there so much evil in the world? Either He can't stop it or He won't stop it; either way, He's not much of a God. And don't quote me the Bible; every cult and world religion has its own book. That's just a self-validating circular argument. Don't talk to me about faith and religion; that's stuff for intellectual wimps. You guys need to get out of the Dark Ages. Science has disproved all that stuff. Look, evolution is true, the Bible is false. Deal with it!"

They looked at me, hurt, and said that a personal relationship with Jesus wasn't about all that; it was about faith. To me, all that meant was that they believed in something they felt deeply but had no reason to know it was true. They just hoped it was. Like Mark Twain, I thought faith was "believing what you know ain't so."

But the Christians had this annoying habit of not getting the hint. Or maybe they were just determined, as if it was a matter of life and death. They'd always come back for more. That was true about the Jesus freaks in high school, and it was true about the Christians on the Reds' team. One of the guys would sit down next to me and start to "share." I'd blast my stock questions. He'd leave and come back with some responses but rarely any answers. I'd ask more questions. He'd leave and return with a couple of reinforcements. They'd all gang up on me, sometimes as many as four on one.

I believe they called this "fellowship," which sounded quite odd to me. Our fellowship never got into big arguments; they were too nice for that. This little dance went on for five seasons. They were great guys. I loved hanging out with them. It's just that they were a little too naive, gullible, and uneducated to be talking to me about religion.

Of course, that would all begin to change for me one night in Dodger Stadium.

23

★ ★ ★

THE SMALLEST GUY ON THE TEAM

On May 30, 1981, a Saturday, a nationally televised game was scheduled against the Dodgers in Los Angeles. Gina had joined me on the flight from Cincinnati to LA on Thursday because she was eight months pregnant, and we wanted her to have the baby at home in Upland, where her parents could help out. She started having contractions on the plane, which was a problem; she wasn't due for another month. We took her to San Antonio Community Hospital as soon as we landed.

She gave birth to our son, Frankie, about 3:15 PM on Friday afternoon. I was in the delivery room, my hands the first to touch my son. He was beautiful, with all his fingers and toes . . . but his coloring was ashen.

The pediatrician, a close friend of Gina's father, took the baby from me. Born four weeks early, Frankie had a condition called hyaline membrane, meaning his lungs were not yet fully developed. Dr. Merrell instructed the nurse to prepare emergency ambulance transport to Queen of the Valley Medical Center, a neonatal facility that specialized in cases such as this. It was about 30 miles away.

Gina had to stay behind. She didn't know what the problem was.

I could hear her crying, "What's wrong with my baby? What's wrong with my baby?"

Her dad and I raced toward the parking lot and jumped in our car to follow the ambulance with its lights flashing. We sped down Interstate 10 to the hospital. The doctors wouldn't let me see my son for more than an hour. When I finally did, his tiny body was punctured by needles and tubes, lying in an incubator under heavy oxygen. The doctors said he had a 50-50 chance of making it through the first week, and that there was nothing we could do but wait.

I still had to get to the ballpark and tell John McNamara what was going on. Dad Pignotti and I drove to Dodger Stadium that Friday night, and I told Mac what had happened.

Mac said, "Go be with your son, and it's your choice if you want to start tomorrow or not."

Dad and I stayed at the hospital all night. There was no improvement.

By Saturday morning, Dad and I were exhausted. We drove back home so I could see Gina. It was heartbreaking. She was so young and had just given birth to her first child, yet she couldn't even hold him. All she had was the news that he had a 50-50 chance of surviving. We cried together, and then Dad and I took off back to see Frankie.

I was an emotional zombie. I didn't know how to even think about the decision to pitch a Major League Baseball™ game on national television while my son was in a life-or-death situation. When we got to the hospital, and I had a chance to see Frankie in that incubator again, the nurses had lightened things up a bit. They'd put up a sign on his incubator that said, "Good luck, Daddy!" That made my decision about playing easier. I knew I had to pitch. I was able to scrub up and, though it was through hospital gloves, finally stroke my son.

The doctors reassured me that he was stable, and so Dad and I took off for the ballpark. As soon as I got there, I went right in to see Mac.

"How is he?" he asked.

"Stable, but they say it's still 50-50 that he'll make it through the week," I said. "Mac, even though I've been up all night, I want to start. It seems like it's the most normal thing I can do right now with all this going on."

With that I started crying again.

"Okay," he said, "but I'll keep a close eye on you. If you want to come out at any time, you just let me know, okay?"

"Okay," I agreed.

By now, reporters and journalists were abuzz about the drama. Years later, players still ask me how I did it. I don't know. I pitched well enough to last $7^{1}/_{3}$ innings and get the win. I don't remember a single thing about it other than wanting to get the game over as soon as possible so that I could return to my son.

In spite of his tough start, Frankie's lungs developed normally, and we were able to bring him home after two weeks in the hospital. He was going to be just fine.

But Frankie's at-risk birth shook me. His little life was so precious, so fragile, and yet he was able to jolt me out of the big, strong material world in which I'd been living. Yeah, the trappings of success were fun, but this tiny guy was more important than all of that. This was life and death—a flesh-and-blood situation—and Frankie pulled at something inside of me.

I began to realize, in a way that I couldn't or wouldn't even articulate, that I may have had all the external signs of success, but there was something wrong. Something was missing. There was a hole in my life that "more" wasn't filling. I tried to fool myself that the next good game, the next sports car, the next winning season, or the next big contract would do the job—but they never did. I began to lose faith that baseball would ever make me happy and fulfilled.

I remember looking around the clubhouse at the players one day, and I suddenly realized that though most of these men had become rich and famous, only a few were truly happy. That was very disturbing. Ever since I was nine years old, I had wanted to be just like them, but if they weren't happy with all of the money and all of the success they had, what made me think I was going to be any different?

The only guys on the team who seemed to be "together" were the guys I regularly made fun of behind their backs: those religious fanatics who brought the Bible into the locker room and along on road trips, those born-again Jesus freaks who believed in the Easter Bunny, Santa Claus, and Somebody rising from the dead.

But as my baby son's health improved, I pulled out of my reflective mood. Gina was thrilled to be a mom. I was pitching decently, and we felt as though we were back in control of our lives. Time went by, and life was good. Of course, I didn't know that just around the next curve, our happy little journey was about to be shattered.

24

★ ★ ★

THE CASE AGAINST CHRIST: NO PROBLEM

Ah, yes, it was June 4, 1984, a clear blue day in the most beautiful park in baseball. We had just scored a few runs, and I was carrying a 3-1 lead into the bottom of the eighth. I was six outs away from outpitching the great Fernando Valenzuela in Los Angeles, something rarely done back then.

I threw a 2-1 fastball on the outside part of the plate. When Steve Sax connected and that baseball came rocketing toward me, I didn't have time to do anything but unconsciously react, raising my right arm to protect my face. The impact hurt—a lot—but the worst part was the loose feel of my elbow and the shards of bone, which jostled around like broken glass.

Shock. Silence. Replays on the JumboTron.

But this was baseball. It wasn't as if I was irreplaceable. Here came my buddy Tommy Hume jogging out onto the field to take over the pitching job.

Holding my elbow and cursing in pain, I walked off the field into the dugout and up the runway into the clubhouse. Right after the game, four of the Christian players—Tommy Hume, Tom Foley,

Duane Walker, and Danny Bilardello—gathered around me in the training room.

"Can we pray for you, Frank?" Humie asked.

"Yeah, you can pray!" I said. "You can do anything you want if you think it'll help."

How cute, I was thinking. *The religious fanatics want to pray for me. People like this always turn to God in crisis situations.*

The only types of prayer I had ever heard were the memorized types, where you basically put your mind on autopilot and then grab the controls again when you hear the word *amen.* Prayer was like singing the national anthem, saying the ABCs, or reciting the Pledge of Allegiance.

But when these guys prayed, it was different. They spoke as if Jesus Christ was real, and that He could not only hear them but was right there with us in that sweaty training room. That was spooky. I had never heard grown men pray as if they really meant it. I may have had all kinds of arguments against Christianity in my head, but right then, my heart wanted to know more about this Jesus they were talking to.

Maybe there is something truly supernatural, something suprascientific, about this God stuff, I thought. It was one thing to raise impersonal intellectual objections against Christianity, as I had done my whole life, but it was another to see teammates you've lived with for the past six years really talking to the Jesus your arguments say doesn't exist.

My elbow was swollen like the Goodyear Blimp that was hovering over Dodger Stadium. The team doctors poked, pulled, and tortured me as best they could and then decided it was best to send me back to Cincinnati for X-rays and diagnostics, since we had just started a two-week road trip. Gina was pregnant with our second child. She took little Frankie back to our home in Upland, and I flew to Cincinnati alone.

There I was, without my wife and best friend, Gina, without my son, with no friends or teammates, and my career possibly over. I was physically, emotionally, and psychologically wounded. I couldn't have been more vulnerable and humbled—or more open to spiritual things. The God-who-wasn't-there had my undivided attention.

On one hand, I couldn't get my teammates' prayer out of my mind. Who was this Jesus, really? On the other hand, I'd been taught to doubt God's existence for as long as I could remember. Christianity was a stupid myth. The universe had popped into existence out of nothing, evolution was a scientific fact, and the Bible was a patched-together human document. I'd been taught that religion was obsolete and that scientists and philosophers like Darwin, Freud, Hume, and Kant had found truth for the modern age.

But I was still drawn to the quality of life I'd seen in those Christians. When I found myself wanting to yield to my emotions and pray, I had to remind myself that God wasn't real. He was merely a crutch for intellectual weaklings, an excuse for mediocrity and failure, a placebo for psychologically imbalanced people . . . but not for this whining, egotistical, and injured professional athlete.

In Cincinnati, the team doctors told me that since nothing was broken, my arm should be "just fine in a few days. It's just some deep bruising and swelling." I kept telling them that I could feel stuff moving around in my elbow, that it didn't feel right, and that I didn't think I could pitch. They said that I was overreacting, that it was "all in my head," and that I would probably just miss a start or two.

I had signed a three-year contract going into the 1984 season and

wanted to pitch well to prove to the Reds, the fans, and my teammates that I was worth every dime they were paying me. Going into
the game in Dodger Stadium, I hadn't been pitching well. I was just
2-4 with a mediocre 4.68 ERA. And of course, right when I had
thrown seven strong innings in LA, and it looked as if I had turned
the corner and was getting my mojo back, I got hit with the line
drive.

I was conflicted. Physically I knew my elbow wasn't right. Psychologically I wanted to get back on the mound and continue pitching well. Maybe the doctors were right. Maybe it was all in my head.

I agreed to take the mound just 11 days after getting drilled. I got
hammered in Atlanta. Then I got hammered in San Diego. Then I
got hammered in San Francisco. Then I got hammered in New York.
I got hammered for the rest of the year.

I kept complaining that my arm wasn't right, but the doctors
wouldn't back me up. But the stats didn't lie. I thought everyone must
be whispering, "He's not pitching well, and he's just blaming it on his
elbow. What a head case." Even I started to believe the whispers—but
the fact was, once I got hit in LA, my elbow was never the same.

Spiritually I was in even worse shape. Since the guys had prayed for
me, I couldn't get the Jesus stuff out of my mind. "What's wrong with
these people?" I grumbled to myself. "They need some serious help." If
I was going to be miserable, I wanted to make sure they were too.

A few weeks after my injury, Tommy Hume, the Reds' chapel
leader, invited me over to his house for a barbecue and a Bible study.
Tommy had asked me many times over the years, and I had always
come up with an excuse.

But this time I agreed.

I arrived at Tommy's house and said hello to the usual suspects, the same guys who had prayed for me in the clubhouse: Humie, Duane Walker, Tom Foley, and Danny Bilardello. I was also introduced to a guy named Wendel Deyo. (They didn't tell me he was the national director of Athletes in Action, a ministry of Campus Crusade, and a 20-year veteran of working with overpaid, prima-donna, insecure professional athletes.)

After the hamburger thing was over, we got down to business. I had never been to a Bible study. I didn't own a Bible. The only one I'd ever seen was the size of Texas, enshrined on a coffee table in an unused living room, with someone's Italian grandmother shrieking, "Don't touch it! It's the *Bible*!"

But still, I knew all about the Bible. I knew it was unhistorical, it contradicts itself, you can make it say anything you want to, and it's been changed many times over the past 2,000 years. So as soon as the opening prayer ended with "amen," I came out shooting. I launched all of my hurt, anger, and confusion in a salvo of blasphemous missiles. I fired for half an hour, attacking all the ridiculous claims of Christianity. The guys just sat and took it, their hair blowing straight back in the hot wind of my tirade.

When I felt I'd successfully enlightened the group, I finally stopped spewing.

Wendel spoke up. "Wow, I've never heard anyone articulate views with such passion and reason as you've just done, Frank. I simply can't answer most of the issues you've raised. I didn't even understand most of 'em! The guys had told me you were smart, but they didn't tell me you were this smart!"

With my good arm I was patting myself on the back.

"But Frank," Wendel continued, waving to the rest of the guys, "we don't want to believe in myths, stories, or anything that isn't true or real either. We're just like you. We want to believe in what's true. Right, guys?"

"Right!" they answered in chorus.

"So, will you help us?" he asked, placing the bait before me.

"Of course. You're my friends. I don't want you guys building your lives on lies," I said magnanimously.

"Great," Wendel replied. "Here's how you can help us. I happen to have brought some books." He grabbed some paperbacks off the floor.

"These books present Christianity better than we can. Will you have a look at them and maybe write in the margins where the authors are wrong and why? Then, after the next road trip, we can all get together again. Then maybe you can enlighten us and we can become happy and fulfilled, just like you!"

"Sure," I said. "I'm glad to help. Really, guys, disproving Christianity won't be very hard. I'll start with Genesis, and we'll just go through and I'll show you why the creation story is an unscientific myth."

In short, I swallowed the bait, hook, line, sinker, pole, and dock.

Wendel handed me three books. I had never met an intelligent Christian before—I thought the term was an oxymoron like "jumbo shrimp." In the past, whenever I would ask Christians a serious question, they would invariably respond, "I can't answer that. You just gotta believe. And anyway, remember, Jesus loves you!"

That never helped me much. I didn't know who Jesus was supposed to be. Nor did it give me the impression that Christianity was rational. But now, since I was going to help this poor, misdirected group achieve enlightenment, I accepted Wendel's books. They were *Mere Christianity* by C. S. Lewis, *Evidence That Demands a Verdict* by

Josh McDowell, and a book on science and origins of the universe from a Christian perspective.

That evening I began reading the shortest one of the three, *Mere Christianity*. I read all night. The next day at the ballpark, I snuck off the bench during the game and hid in the weight room to continue reading.

Over the next few weeks I read and reread the books. I devoured them. The Christian guys touched base with me a few times to ask how things were going. I told them that I was still working on disproving the Bible but that it was just taking a little longer than I expected.

25

★ ★ ★

SURRENDER IN THE MEN'S ROOM

This whole Christian thing was really bothering me. Even though I knew my mother's training was not to be trusted, it was hard to shake it off. Religion was stupid. We were smarter than that. Only naive and gullible people fell for faith in something you couldn't see. Of course, it had never entered my mind that I had completely dismissed Christianity without having the slightest idea what Christians really believed.

As I read C. S. Lewis's *Mere Christianity*, I began to get a taste of that. *Whoa*, I thought. *This guy was obviously smart. He was a professor at Oxford. How'd he get sucked into this Christian thing?*

So I continued to read. Lewis was brilliant, captivating, intriguing. Everything I had come to think Christians were not. Gradually I began to consider, for the first time, that this stuff could actually possibly be true. If it was, then that meant everything else was different from my lifelong assumptions.

For years I'd been a practicing nihilist, assuming that there was no particular meaning to anything and that our time on earth was simply about amassing the most pleasures you could before you passed on to nothingness. I had stuff that made me feel secure—cars, clothes, money—I was a fun guy who could pick up the tab for all my fun friends. I had a job I loved and the Major League™ respect that came with it. Like any half-decent baseball player, I was a hero. Kids would approach me, their eyes shining, and ask me to sign their baseball cards. The media sought me out too; reporters knew I was good for a colorful quote. And, miracle of miracles, I had a beautiful wife who really loved me, a son who'd survived a tough birth and was now flourishing, and another baby on the way.

But, as I'd thought before but never allowed myself to really consider, the problem was that no matter how much I had, it was never enough. No matter how much stuff I had, I wanted more. No matter how many good write-ups I got, or how much cheering I heard in the stands, it was never quite enough.

This was weird, because it presented an unsolvable problem: If feeling good depends on amassing stuff, and you constantly need more stuff to satisfy that craving, then what do you do? How can you ever get enough? I knew way too many stories of rich celebrities who'd blown their brains out or just soaked their minds in alcohol or drugs so they wouldn't feel the pain of the endless quest for more.

What if the whole game is set up differently? I thought. *What if the rules I thought were right are actually wrong? What if there's a bigger story here?*

My encounter with Jesus wasn't based, initially, on personal conviction. It wasn't that I felt I'd hit bottom and needed Him to fish me out. It wasn't that I felt so bad about my sin and needed deliverance. Those realizations would come later.

No, at the beginning of my spiritual interest, encountering Christ was all about the relentless logic of the Big Story, not my personal story. Through Lewis's writing I began to see that there really was a God, that He created humanity with free will, that His heart broke over the severed relationship with people who wanted to go their own way. I saw that He made a way to restore that relationship, through Jesus. I saw that in the end of the Big Story, good will absolutely triumph over evil.

I began to believe that this Big Story was true and real and compelling. It made sense, as opposed to chasing stuff all my life like a rat on a wheel, stuff that could never truly satisfy. *I want to sign up for this*, I thought. *I want to make this team. I want to be on the side that wins.*

It was a subtle shift. No big whooping or drama. I just arrived at the point where my mind and heart locked in on a new way of thinking. I knew Christianity was true.

So now I needed to figure out, how do I join? Sometimes people put so much emphasis on this entry point. They talk about "getting saved" as if that's the end of the story. But that's like confusing the wedding with the marriage. The wedding establishes the relationship between the bride and the groom. It's the entry point. The marriage is the ongoing story of the relationship.

So I decided I wanted to sign up. Get on the team. Commit to the relationship.

My injury happened on June 4. On Saturday, August 25, we had a night game in Pittsburgh. I had been constantly sneaking away from the team to read my new books, and that day was no exception. I made the formal decision to join the team in the clubhouse bathroom— second stall from the right—reading.

Yep, I was sitting there on the commode perusing Josh McDowell's book *Evidence That Demands a Verdict*. Chapter 7. Josh sums up C. S. Lewis's argument that there were only three possibilities as to who Jesus Christ really was.

He could have been a liar—an all-out counterfeit determined to convince everyone that He was God, even though He wasn't. Or He could have been a lunatic—a crazy person suffering from tragic delusions of grandeur. Or He was telling the truth.

Considering the actual evidence of the case, common sense and reason would lead most thoughtful people to conclude that Jesus was telling the truth.

And then, there, in that lowly stall, I got it. *Whoa!* I thought. *If this is true—and it is—then I want it!*

At the end of the chapter, there was a prayer you could pray if you wanted to follow Jesus. Still sitting there on the commode, I prayed silently, "Lord, I want to be on Your team. I'm not crazy about some of the people who are on it, and I'm not crazy about some of the stuff that is done in Your name. But I want to commit my life to You."

I stood up and flushed, a new person in Christ. All my stinking sins had been washed away. I went back into the clubhouse. By now the game was over, and we had lost, 5-3. The locker room was quiet, as it always is after a loss. I went over behind my buddy Tommy Hume, one of the Christians who'd been praying for me and giving me books.

"Humie," I whispered to him, "I just prayed to receive Christ."

He whipped around to face me. "Praise the Lord!" he said, a little too loudly.

The players nearby turned to stare. I had been pitching poorly for weeks since the injury, and they all knew I was "getting religion," reading those weird books all the time and hanging out with the Christians way too much.

"Shh, Tommy, not so loud," I said. "Let's talk about this back at the hotel."

I was excited about Jesus, but I didn't want to be associated with religion or weird spiritual yelling. I didn't want to get labeled as a fundamentalist wacko. A lot of guys on the team were just like I had been—they thought Christians were serious nut jobs.

Later, all the Christian guys on the team gathered in Tommy's hotel room. I was the last one to arrive. I closed the door behind me, locked it, and looked at them. They looked back at me, grinning and expectant.

In my usual fashion, I didn't lack for self-confidence, even though it wasn't warranted.

"Guys!" I said. "For years you've been sharing with me why I needed to become a Christian. I've been asking you all these basic questions, like why do you believe God exists, how do you know the Bible is true, why is there evil in the world, why is Christianity the only true religion, what about the person who's never heard of Jesus— and for more than five years you've given me really *bad* answers. I could have *died* and gone to *hell*, and my *blood* would have been on *your* hands!"

They all stared at me, wishing they had focused their evangelistic attentions on someone else. Someone nicer. If they had expected that my long-sought conversion would have produced a kinder, gentler Frank, they were wrong.

26

★ ★ ★

END OF A DREAM

I may have been hard on my fellow Christians right after my conversion, but I loved them—and miraculously enough, they'd been loving me for years. That's what drew me to actually consider Christ in the first place.

In my new way of thinking, I also loved the Bible. It was wild; after so many years of dismissing it out of hand, I was astonished to find how intriguing it really was. I would read long chunks in the New Testament, and Christ was totally different from who I thought He was. So wise, so surprising, so cool. I saw how the Old Testament foreshadowed His coming. I loved the big picture.

Wendel Deyo gave me my first Bible, a big, honkin' Ryrie Study Bible with lots of notes, maps, commentary, and other research tools. I couldn't get enough of it. Wendel also told me how important it was that I share my "testimony" with people.

I found out that my testimony was the story of how I came to believe in Jesus. I was thrilled to let people know about that; just let me at 'em. One of the first places I did this was at Cedarville University in Ohio. The president had gathered the student body together, and I was supposed to give a five-minute testimony before the real speaker they had lined up.

I came out onto the stage, my enormous Bible under my arm, and I told those kids about my unlikely transition from being an atheist to being a Christian. I couldn't shut up. After a while the guys who brought me tried to pull me off the stage, but I went on and on, maybe 45 minutes, until I had told them my whole story.

The kids loved it though.

In those early days of being a believer, I was also learning about "fellowship." I'd travel to different cities with the Reds, and in each one, miraculously, there were these Christians crawling out of the woodwork, wanting to get together with me for lunch and talk about faith.

"This is really wild," I told Wendel. "There must be a real moving of the Spirit in all these places where we happen to be playing." Later, of course, I realized that he had contacted Christians in the cities I was traveling to, asking them to encourage me in the faith. It worked.

I had new ears for baseball chapel speakers as well. One time we had this amazing godly speaker who did a talk for the team in the clubhouse in Atlanta. Afterward I got ahold of Wendel. "Hey," I told him, "that guy was really good. You should use him for other Christian stuff like this." Later I realized the speaker had been Charles Stanley, and he already had plenty of speaking gigs on his plate.

Meanwhile, Gina wasn't sure what to make of her new "religious" husband. When I came home from the road trip to Pittsburgh, she thought that my eyes looked different the moment I walked off the plane. Then, me being me, the first words I uttered to my beloved were "I asked Jesus into my life, and you need to accept Him too!"

Not a recommended start with your unbelieving spouse.

Gina immediately concluded that her husband had become a

religious fanatic. As I told her about how Tommy Hume and the other players had challenged me to accept the case for Christ, all she could say was, "But Frank! We are Christians! We're Catholic! And I will *always* be Catholic!"

Gina didn't know who I was anymore. She began to feel panicky. One of the first things I did when I got home was to throw away my big pile of *Playboy* magazines. Then while I was out doing errands, Gina went to the garbage can, pulled out the magazines, and put them in a neat stack on my dresser.

When I asked her about it, she said she'd saved them just in case the new Frank was only temporary. I told her the new Frank was here to stay, and I wasn't into that stuff anymore. She said there was nothing wrong with viewing these "adult magazines" and even argued that God created sex, so they were fine. I couldn't believe I was having this conversation with my wife.

As Gina remembers it, she felt as if our old familiar life was slipping away, and she was trying to hold on to anything she could. Today, of course, she feels it was extremely odd that she wasn't glad I no longer wanted to view and fantasize over naked women. I'd told her that the only woman I wanted to experience these things with was her—and yet here was Gina, digging the porn out of the trash. It didn't make any sense, but Gina says that the Holy Spirit had begun to work on her, and she was resisting God's changes in our lives in any way she could.

Later we burned the *Playboy*s in the fireplace—together.

At the time, though, Gina thought it was just a phase. Whenever I did interviews, now I was proclaiming my new beliefs and sharing the gospel. She nearly died of embarrassment. She'd been raised to keep matters of faith private. Civilized people just didn't discuss religion or politics. Though she'd loved her Catholic faith as a young girl, she'd slipped away from her religious upbringing and just didn't find it interesting anymore.

I asked Gina to come with me to a Bible study that some of the players and their wives attended. We were at the home of Cincinnati Bengals' player Anthony Muñoz, and Wendel Deyo was leading a study on prayer. Gina told him how she'd been taught to pray to the Virgin Mary and various saints. Wendel told her that the Bible doesn't teach these practices and that in the Scripture God directs His people to pray directly to Him. Gina told him crisply that she'd check into it further. She was angry, frustrated, convicted, and resisting God at every turn.

A few weeks later, while I was away with the Reds on a road trip, Gina was at home with Frankie. She was six months pregnant with our second child, and there was a knock at the door. Gina opened it to discover Wendel Deyo and Anthony Muñoz, all six feet eight of him. Surprised, she invited them in.

Wendel didn't beat around the bush. "Well, Gina," he said, "we were just wondering if you'd checked into those things we talked about at the Bible study. Is there anything you want to talk about?"

This guy just doesn't give up, does he? Gina said to herself.

They all sat down at the dining-room table. Gina told them she liked praying to Mary. That was how she was brought up, and it gave her comfort. Wendel looked her straight in the eyes, pointed to his Bible, and said, "Well, Gina, either you believe this Book or you don't. It's totally your decision, but you've got to make it."

Gina looked at Wendel. She realized she did believe the Book, but she wasn't ready to surrender her life completely to God. It was as if her head was saying yes but her heart was saying no.

But even though she was still resisting, something had changed. As she puts it, "I knew the truth now. Even though I didn't like it, I knew it was true. I began to surrender myself to God slowly over the course of about a year."

For Gina, a big step in that surrender actually came when she was giving birth to our daughter at the end of October 1984. The delivery was tough, and she made a personal pact with God: "You get me through this, and I will completely surrender my life to Christ. And as a marker of that, I will name this baby in His honor."

And that, of course, is how our daughter, Christina, got her name.

Wendel had told us that the way to grow as new believers was to digest the Bible on a daily basis, to pray, to find a good church, and to share our faith with others. Since I'd come from a totally secular background, considering the idea of going to church was weird to me. Given Gina's strong Catholic feelings, when we returned home to Upland for the off-season, we went to the Catholic church in our parish.

To me it felt like ritual without real meaning, like everyone was just going through the motions, the priest included. I met with him and asked if we could get some Bible studies going. The priest put his hand on my shoulder. "Son, you're still young," he told me. "This religious enthusiasm you're feeling right now is just a phase; you'll grow out of it."

I stared at him in disbelief for a moment before walking out of his office, confused and disappointed. I couldn't understand how a man who would commit himself to celibacy in order to serve God didn't want other people studying His Book. It didn't make sense.

That's when Pam Lahr, Gina's Christian friend who lived across the street, invited us to come to church with her. Pam knew that I would hit it off with her pastor, since he was a former professional athlete. Ray Schmautz had been a linebacker with the Oakland Raiders years earlier, before starting a Bible study that grew into Life Bible Fellowship, the church Pam attended. We went, we did hit it off, and our family attended LBF for years. Ray helped lay a solid foundation for my Christian faith. And many of our close friendships today can be traced back to those early years at LBF.

Even as Gina and I were growing stronger in our faith, together, things were getting worse, not better, on the baseball front. The injury to my pitching arm didn't end my career in a blaze of glory, all at once. No, it took me down slowly, painfully, and with a good deal of humiliation. I pitched another 13 games in the 1984 season, after the injury on June 4 of that year. In 1985, I pitched 17 games from the season opener until mid-July, when I finally had surgery.

During those 30 games—a long and terrible interim—I tried all kinds of things to compensate for my pain and increasing ineffectiveness. Nothing would bring back the zip and movement on the ball that I once had. I tried all kinds of new pitches, different grips, even a "hurry-up" windup that I'm still embarrassed about today.

The hitters loved me. I had become a batting-practice pitcher. It was emotionally devastating to once have been so good and now be so bad. I dreaded having to pitch. My arm was killing me, all the time. It hurt to comb my hair, let alone throw a baseball hard enough to strike out Major League™ hitters. I had once gone into battle with superior weaponry, and now I was marching into inevitable slaughter. Every time.

It's hard to mentally compete at the highest level when you know you don't have it physically anymore. I pulled the trigger so many times, hoping to fire a bullet and getting only a dud. Then I realized all I had were duds, and I didn't want to pull the trigger anymore.

My last game in the National League was a home game against Montreal on July 12, 1985. I had pitched five innings and was holding on to a 5-4 lead. My elbow hurt so bad I couldn't continue. The Reds flew me out to LA to be examined by Dr. Frank Jobe.

Dr. Jobe showed me the X-rays, which indicated a lot of calcium deposits and bone chips in the joint. When I came out of surgery, he told me it was the dirtiest pitcher's elbow he had ever worked on. The Sax line drive had broken off pieces of bone that had been floating around in my elbow for the past year. He was surprised I could pitch at all, given the debris in my arm and the level of pain.

After all the doubts and team whispers that I'd started to believe, the medical truth was that the problems with my pitching arm were indeed real. They hadn't been in my head. It was an immense relief to realize that.

Back home in Upland, I recovered from the surgery. I was still drawing my paychecks from the Reds. Gina and I continued to go to Life Bible Fellowship. Baby Christina was now a toddler, and little Frankie was going to start school in September. We were all growing in various ways.

Meanwhile, back at the Cincinnati Reds, a guy named Pete Rose was breaking the all-time hit record. Pete, of course, was a phenomenon. He'd been signed by the Reds back in 1960, celebrated his 3,000th career hit in 1978, and became a free agent in 1979, signing with the Philadelphia Phillies in a contract that made him the highest-paid athlete in team sports at the time. He'd played for the Montreal Expos for a year, becoming the second player in history—after Ty Cobb—to make 4,000 hits. Pete had come back to the Reds in August 1984 and was immediately named player-manager, replacing Vern Rapp.

On September 11, 1985, Pete broke Ty Cobb's all-time hits

record with his 4,192nd hit. ABC's *Wide World of Sports* named Rose Athlete of the Year. So at the time our paths came together, Pete was incredibly famous, rich, and powerful. Meanwhile, I was, shall we say, not at the high point of my career. But I had a higher love than baseball now, so I was witnessing to just about anything that moved, including Pete Rose.

Pete was not amused.

I missed the rest of the 1985 season after undergoing surgery in July, but by the time spring training rolled around in February 1986, I was almost up to full strength. I was in the middle of a guaranteed contract, which meant I was going to get paid $450,000 for the year whether I played or not. I just wanted to get healthy enough to maybe return to the rotation and take my turn every fifth day. Pete had told me that I would likely start the year in long relief and that I could work my way back into the rotation from there.

But as spring went on, the sportswriters started floating rumors about me getting traded. The traditional wisdom was that as a veteran of seven Major League™ seasons, I could certainly contribute in the bull pen, even in the mop-up role, but no new team would be interested in a trade since it was uncertain whether my arm was yet healthy. So I had settled on the idea of probably pitching out of the bull pen, just as Pete had said.

I had mixed outings, some good, some bad, but mostly just okay. With only about a week to go before the Reds' moving truck went north from Tampa with players' personal belongings on it, I remember specifically asking Pete whether I should put my family's stuff on the van to Cincinnati.

He just laughed. "Of course," he said. "You're a veteran. What am I going to do, release you?"

Gina and I loaded up our kids' stuff in the trunks and brought our belongings to the ballpark. A few days later, now with just two days to go before we broke camp, I pitched three innings in Florida's Dunedin Stadium against the Toronto Blue Jays and gave up a few runs.

When we got back to Tampa, I looked around the clubhouse. Guys' faces were closed; they wouldn't quite make eye contact. It was unsettling. Then our clubby Bernie Stowe approached my locker in such a way that I knew exactly what was about to happen. I had seen it many times over the past 12 years.

"Pete wants to see you in his office, kid," he said in a sad voice.

A buzz went through the locker room. Everybody watched me walk to Pete's office. Seated there along with Pete Rose was Jim Kaat (aka "Kitty"), the pitching coach, and Scotty Breeden, the minor-league pitching instructor.

I sat in the one empty chair in that tiny office.

"Frank," Pete said without preliminaries, "I'm releasing you."

I heard those words, and then words I hadn't even planned started rolling out of me. "Well, Pete," I said, "I want to thank you for the privilege of playing with you. I'll be able to tell my grandkids about it. And Scotty and Kitty, thanks for everything. I owe much of my life to baseball, and it was great while it lasted. And Pete, I just wish you had told me the truth the other day so I wouldn't have sent all that stuff to Cincinnati on the moving truck!"

I was emotional but still in control.

Pete got visibly upset. "Don't you want to hit me or something?" he asked, irritated by my calm.

"Hit you?" I asked. "For what? You're just making what you think is the best decision for the team, that's all."

That really got him going. "See?" he yelled. "That's what's wrong with you. No passion anymore. You've got all this talent, and you got hurt. This God s— isn't going to help you! So many guys get into religion and this Bible s—. This game of life is about looking out for number one. It's dog eat dog. Eat or be eaten. And here you are with all this 'Jesus loves you' crap. I just don't get it." He paused for a couple of seconds and then went on. "How can you really believe that God crap? Answer me this, if there's a God, why are there retarded children?"

"Pete," I said, "I don't know why God allows retarded children. I don't know why bad things happen to good people. But I do know that God has a plan for everything, including my life and yours. Why do you think He chose you, out of all the players in the world, to be the one to break Ty Cobb's record? I'm going to pray for you."

He looked at me as if I were from another planet. A planet he hated. He just sat there shaking his head. Scotty extended his hand, and I shook it, and Kitty's, but Pete wouldn't even look at me. So I turned and walked out of his office with my head held high.

Pete eventually ran into troubles of his own. He soon left baseball, ineligible to play for life, under a cloud of accusations that he'd been betting on games. He began therapy with a psychiatrist for a gambling addiction and later pled guilty to two charges of filing false income-tax returns, spent time in prison, and paid heavy fines.

But of course I wouldn't know any of that until later. When Pete fired me, I had a strange peace about the whole thing, even as I walked out of his office. Maybe it was spiritual. Or maybe I was just so completely cut off from my emotions that I was having an out-of-body experience, as if it wasn't really happening to me, but I was watching it happen to someone else.

Really down deep I must have known it was coming. I'd been an outsider to this team since my surgery, and now it was official. My friends came over, many with tears in their eyes, to say good-bye. I packed up my gear, made the rounds, and walked out of that clubhouse, where I had spent 11 years of my life. Before heading back to Gina, I wanted to stop by Redsland, our spring-training complex, for one last visit.

I walked into the empty clubhouse. The players had gone for the day.

"Who's that?" a voice from the coach's office called out. I walked over to find my first manager, Jimmy Hoff, sitting there filling out reports. Jimmy was a good man.

"Hey, Jimmy," I said, "I just wanted to see the place one more time before leaving. Pete just released me."

Jimmy sighed. "I'm sorry to hear that, Frank. You're a good guy. But, hey, that's baseball, right?"

27

★ ★ ★

WHY WE ARE NOT FRIENDS WITH THE IRS

If Pete Rose initiated the beginning of the end of my baseball career, the end of the end came in just a few quick strokes. Three weeks after Pete released me, I got signed by the Minnesota Twins. I played in 33 games for them through the rest of the 1986 season. Afterward, they told my agent they would not be resigning me for the following year. A good decision on their part, since they obviously didn't need me to win the 1987 World Series!

The 1986–1987 off-season was difficult for all free agents. Years later, baseball owners would be found guilty of collusion because they had illegally limited player mobility and salaries. I had done okay with the Twins, good enough to warrant another year in the show. My agent was confident I would sign a two-year deal with the Los Angeles Angels and be able to play at home—a player's dream.

But this wasn't an ordinary year. The phone was ringing only for the best free agents. It wasn't ringing for me.

Spring training started, and I was still at home. A month went by, and my agent got me a walk-on tryout with the Texas Rangers AAA club, the Oklahoma City 89ers (now the Red Hawks), but I'd have to pay my own expenses to get there. I drove from LA to Florida, walked on, tried out, and made the team. I was told I'd be given four starts in AAA. If I didn't excel in those four starts, I'd be released.

Well, I didn't excel, and I was released.

When I got home my agent told me not to worry, that he could still get me a job with another organization here in the States, or maybe a gig in Mexico.

"Frank, you're only 30," he said. "You're still too young to hang 'em up."

I just shook my head. "Nope," I said. "I'm done."

You'd think that leaving the big leagues would have been traumatic. I'd drawn my identity from baseball since I was 9 years old. I'd drawn my paycheck from it since I was 17. Baseball was all I'd known. But I had an odd sense of excitement. It was time to get started with "real life"—whatever that was. It would be like an extended off-season. We'd get to live in one place year round and have dinner together as a family every night.

I probably had visions of Ozzie and Harriet or some other 1960s-ish TV family dancing in my head. I was going to "go to work" somewhere every day in a "real job," come home, hug the children and Gina, who would be wearing pearls and a little apron, and then we'd eat a healthy, well-balanced dinner.

Plus, I was a Christian now. I knew God had great plans for us. I couldn't wait to find out what they were.

It was May 1987. Frankie was six, in kindergarten, and Christina was two and a half. We had pretty good investments, a modest home that was paid off, a little money in the bank, and a paid-off Porsche and Mercedes in the driveway.

My brother-in-law and I had started a construction company. He was the general contractor; I was going to get my broker's license, and we'd build tract homes. I was ready to live happily ever after. If my life had been a movie, this would have been the natural place for the villain to enter our happy scene.

He did—in the form of the Internal Revenue Service.

One day I went out to our mailbox, and behold, there was a letter from the IRS. It stated in no uncertain terms that Gina and I owed the United States government four hundred thousand dollars.

We had heard horror stories about people who had cut corners and lost it all, so we were big on paying all our taxes faithfully. We thought we were on great terms with our IRS friends in Washington.

Not so.

It turns out that a bunch of doctors, lawyers, entertainers, and pro athletes like me had made what we thought were legitimate investments. But the principals involved had submitted fraudulent financial papers, claiming to have made transactions on Wall Street that in fact had not transpired. We had relied on the fraudulent information when we filed our tax returns, and now the government was rejecting all those alleged transactions. The IRS was peeved. And it wanted its money in 90 days.

Back then four hundred thousand dollars was big money, particularly for us; it still is. Gone immediately were all the liquid assets, like CDs, bonds, and stocks. We had to sell all our real-estate holdings at a loss, which left us with no rental income. (My mother had lied to me about my name being on the title and "owning" the house in Birmingham, so selling that property wasn't an option.) We sold the Mercedes and the Porsche. We were able to keep our paid-off home in Upland . . . but we lost most everything else.

It was a bucket of ice water in the face.

What am I gonna do? I thought. I had zero college. No real work experience, no job leads. The business execs at the country club liked having me around to tell baseball stories when we played golf, but would any of them hire me? All my life I had been treated like someone special because I could throw stuff hard. I'd made a good living doing just that, but now it was gone with the elbow. Really, I didn't know how to do much of anything other than read and talk.

I called around for advice. Steve Garvey, the former Dodger great, connected me with Professional Athletes Career Enterprises (PACE), a group he founded that retooled pro athletes, like old cars, for new vocations. They ran me through IQ tests, aptitude tests, personality profiles, and vocational tests.

I won't bore you with the particulars of my vocational identity crisis. The result was that they told me I needed to get my college degree as fast as I could, preferably in business, so that I would be a marketable commodity. There just wasn't a big demand right then for high-school-only ex-baseball players.

I applied to National University. I studied like a wild man, took exams that would exempt me from various subjects, and passed 'em all. I started with the equivalent of two years of college credits under my belt.

My first class was Marketing 101, and the students voted that our class project would be how to market a baseball camp for profit. With their help, I was able to put on a great camp. A couple hundred kids, for a whole week, got to learn from great instructors and stars like Mark McGwire, Eric Davis, and Mike Scioscia, and we even had Major League™ umpires work our games.

By the time everyone got paid, I had cleared ten grand. Not bad for a week's work. I was good at teaching kids how to pitch, and a number of parents asked me if I would work one-on-one with their sons. I hadn't even thought of that, but I loved it. I charged one hundred dollars an hour, and word spread. I continued giving pitching lessons for the next 17 years.

Also in that first class, I got recruited by Digital Equipment Corporation. I didn't know diddly about computers. That was okay. Digital didn't want me to actually sell computers; they wanted me to wine and dine their big customers, playing golf with guys, taking them to a few ball games once in a while.

It was a cushy job until management changed. From then on I wasn't doing PR; I had to really sell computer systems. If I didn't excel in the sales training, I'd lose my job. I studied my tail off, won Best Sales Presentation in the competition, and kept my job.

One of my first clients was Campus Crusade for Christ. One day, at their Arrowhead Springs headquarters in San Bernardino, California, they surprised me with a phone call from a "mystery caller." It was the guy who had led me to Christ, Wendel Deyo. All those years I'd known him in Cincinnati, and I'd never realized he was the national director of Athletes in Action, the sports-ministry arm of Campus Crusade. We laughed, caught up with each other, and then Wendel suggested I come on Crusade staff after I graduated from National.

From 1987 through 1989 I worked at Digital from nine to five and went to National two nights a week and every other Saturday; I gave pitching lessons on alternate Saturdays. On Sundays we were at church, if I wasn't out sharing my testimony somewhere on the road. By the time graduation rolled around, I guess my 4.0 GPA had impressed Digital enough that they offered to pay for an MBA under Peter Drucker if I'd stay on with them.

But I really wanted to work in full-time ministry. I'd had a small taste of corporate America, and it was okay, but man, if I could work full-time for the Lord in a big ministry, where everyone would be a Christian, that would be a little taste of heaven. Everyone would get along in perfect harmony, leadership would be godly and wise, and I'd be happy and fulfilled. I just knew it would be wonderful. So I turned down Digital's offer and decided to go on staff with Crusade to work with Wendel at Athletes in Action.

The first big challenge with my new call to ministry was this thing about "raising support." Gina, who was interested in continuing to feed our two growing children, who were now eight and five, was against the whole idea. When I had initially talked about going on staff with Wendel, I'd assumed it would be for a small but livable salary. I didn't know I'd have to go out and ask people for money.

But I was already so emotionally and spiritually invested in the idea of full-time ministry, I really didn't give Gina any choice. She reluctantly agreed. Her parents thought I was nuts. They had never heard of raising support and thought it sounded weird at best and cultish at worst. It was embarrassing to have their son-in-law, once a Major League Baseball™ player, going around town begging people for one hundred dollars a month.

The problem was, I didn't yet have a biblical understanding of work and ministry. I was gung ho for Jesus and thought the best way to serve Him with all my heart was to go into full-time ministry. I also continued to be blown by prevailing winds. I'd been so devoid of wise counsel growing up, and so at a loss for a strong father figure, that I tended to listen to—and impulsively follow—whatever older man I looked up to. Whether it was a teacher, a coach, a manager, or a mentor, I attached easily to people in authority. Often these guys gave me great advice; sometimes, though they weren't consciously manipulating me for bad purposes, they led me down unwise paths. Even though I was 32 years old, I was looking for the mentoring father I never had. My dad taught me to play baseball, but little else. Dad Pignotti loved me and cheered me on, but he didn't really see life and faith in a way that helped me grow. Sometimes I was so hungry for spiritual direction and guidance that—though I wanted to be obedient to God's leading—I followed bad advice.

I was also naive about working in Christian organizations. I'd had no illusions about the seamy side of life in pro sports—I'd seen it all. And I knew that churches and Christian ministries are made up of sinful people—people who've been saved, yes, and are on the road to heaven but who are still vulnerable to the temptations of pride, ego, turf wars, and jealousy. I knew all that intellectually, but I still had a rosy picture in my mind that working in full-time ministry would be different, that it would be somehow elevated, above all the lures of self and sin. Somehow God would protect us because it wasn't "business"; it was ministry.

If my life were a movie, this is where you'd hear more villain music playing ever so faintly in the background. Except this time the bad guy wasn't the IRS.

28

★ ★ ★

WONDERING AS I WANDERED

After the humbling experience of asking friends, neighbors, former colleagues, and family members for monthly support, Gina and I packed up the kids and our stuff. We rented a U-Haul and set out for the house I'd just bought in Cincinnati where I would join Wendel and the staff of Athletes in Action.

I did a lot of chapels with the Bengals and the Reds but found it pretty shallow. The problem was that I was shallow . . . but nevertheless, the same issues always came up over and over again. Players would say, "I'm being unfaithful to my wife. How can I stop?" "What am I going to do with my life when my career is over?" "I'm making all this money, but I feel empty. What's wrong with me?" "Does my wife love me for me or because I'm rich?" "I'm in a slump. Can God fix it?"

Those are valid questions. But I wasn't a counselor, and I didn't like the hand-holding stuff. I was more excited about the fact that Christianity was true and what that meant about the nature of God. I was into more of the big picture, the grand drama of it all, not the kind of mind-set that looks to God as a cosmic vending machine with buttons we can push for all our various needs and problems.

What really turned me on was speaking on college campuses in open forums, where students could ask anything about Christianity. I loved the debate, the give-and-take, and the opportunity to lay out the evidence for faith in the crucible of a university setting. Scheduled half-hour meetings would go on for three hours. I loved it. If only I could make a decent living doing it.

After we'd been in Cincinnati for six months, Crusade leadership called me in to suggest I consider going to seminary. They saw how effective I was on campuses even though I hadn't yet had formal theological training. My heart loved the idea of going to seminary. But my head told me it was time to grow up, go home, and get a real job. Our support was dropping, and we were burning through what little baseball savings we had left. My kids needed clothes, and I was tired of telling my family, "We're in ministry; we don't have enough money for that."

If I'd really been called to that ministry, I believe I would have felt differently. But I'd jumped impulsively into it without counting the cost. Gina and I came to the conclusion that full-time ministry was for other people, not us. I had a family to support, and that was my primary ministry.

Without telling anyone at Crusade, I had already applied to law school back home and was prepping for the LSAT at night. I listened to the Crusade guys' advice, but I knew I'd never go to seminary unless God hit me on the head with a baseball bat.

About a week before we were due to head back home to law school in California, I got a call one night from Danny Carroll, the former youth pastor from our church in Upland. Danny had never called us in Cincinnati, and we had only hung out a few times back home. I didn't know him very well.

After exchanging pleasantries, he got to the point of his call.

"Frank, the Lord told me to tell you something," he said. "I don't know what this means, but He told me to tell you, 'Go to seminary.' Does that mean anything to you?"

It wasn't a baseball bat, but to me it was mind-blowing. No one knew we were leaving other than my direct leadership in Cincinnati, and there was no connection between them and Danny. Nor had we told anyone back in Upland.

"Who told you?" I asked him.

"No one," he said. "I just felt prompted by the Holy Spirit to call you and tell you that."

Danny wouldn't lie. Gina and I took it as a word from the Lord, dropped the idea of going to law school on the spot—though I would wrestle with it from time to time—and made the decision to enroll at nearby Talbot School of Theology, the seminary associated with Biola University in Orange County. When I look back at some of my impulsive decisions, it's a wonder we didn't get whiplash!

When we returned to California in July of 1991, we had to live with Gina's parents, since our house was still leased to a renter for another six months. I started summer classes at Talbot and set up an office in the garage, putting my computer and printer on a folding table. I'd study out there for hours without any air-conditioning.

The kids were stuck in one bedroom, Gina and I got her old bedroom back, and the whole time, her parents thought I was wasting my life on some fantasy. Again. If becoming a "born again" Christian wasn't bad enough and raising support to go on staff with Campus Crusade wasn't embarrassing enough, now I'd gone over the top, spending thousands of our last baseball dollars to go to seminary. I'd gone from being a spiritual wacko to becoming a professional religious nut.

Thanks to Mrs. Pignotti, we ate well every night, but dinners were almost unbearable.

"What are you going to do with your degree when you're done?" Mr. Pignotti would ask. "Where are you going to work? How are you going to feed my grandchildren?"

The worst thing was, I had no real answers. I told them that if God had called me to do this, He'd provide for us, which was true. But down deep, I wasn't sure if God had really called me to chase this seminary dream, or if I was just a human Ping-Pong ball, bouncing from thing to thing to thing.

Dennis Dirks was the Talbot dean, and like the rest of the faculty, he was skeptical about this former baseball player wanting to go to seminary. One day he called me into his office.

"Frank, are you chewing tobacco and using Coke cans to spit in?" he asked.

"Yes, sir," I said.

"Well, you need to stop," he said, smiling, knowing it was fairly ridiculous for the dean of a seminary to have to confront a student about chewing tobacco.

"Okay," I said cooperatively. And I did stop. I stopped being so careless with my spittoons. I became much more discreet. I started washing them out before throwing them in the trash can.

After a year of observation of everything from my spittoon habits to my academic pursuits, the dean called me back into his office one day.

"Frank, when you finish Talbot, what do you plan on doing?" Dennis asked.

"I'd like to teach," I said.

Then he asked, "With your diverse background, let me ask you a question. What is it that you think Talbot needs to be doing to make a bigger impact?"

I thought for a moment. "Three things. First, you need to do some large, free events here on campus, because most of the churches don't know who you are or what you do. Second, you need to send your best instructors into churches to teach classes that will minister to the laypeople directly. Bring the seminary to them. And third, you need to get back on national radio with a live show that addresses the news of the day from a Christian worldview."

Dennis smiled and said, "How would you like to head up the program that does those three things?"

I couldn't believe it! Without knowing it, I had outlined my dream job, and now this guy was offering it to me.

29

★ ★ ★

WHEN THE BLUEBIRDS SANG

"Unfortunately," Dean Dirks continued, "we don't have any money to do any of these things. But if you can find a way to raise the money, or find a way to generate enough revenue to pay yourself a small salary, then maybe this can work."

My wheels started turning.

I had soured on the whole living-on-support thing with Campus Crusade, but I believed this could be different if I was more in control. Since Biola wasn't paying me a salary, it was more like they were allowing me to start my own ministry with their covering. It seemed like the best of both worlds. I would be in full-time ministry while still giving pitching lessons in the afternoons, teaching in the program at night, and doing conferences and retreats on the weekends. If I set this up right, it could work.

Our first on-campus event was a conference called Jesus Under Fire in 1995. It addressed some of the current cultural fallacies about Jesus, and it drew 3,000 people on the Biola campus. A big success.

I got a few other guys to join me, and we started TIBS, the Talbot Institute of Biblical Studies, a program of six-week courses held one night a week in local churches, taught by the best instructors I could find. We covered all kinds of topics, from Christian worldview to cults to world religions to doctrines, such as the nature of God and the problem of evil. We charged only $40 per adult, and we let high school students sit in for free. When students completed 16 classes, Talbot would issue them a certificate. I paid the instructors $200 a night for two hours of teaching, and they could sell their books. To break even required 30 paying students per class; anything beyond that went to overhead and a paltry salary for me. I taught three times a week throughout the whole program.

Over the next four years, more than 6,000 paying adults took at least one of our TIBS classes in 26 churches in the Greater Los Angeles area. Thousands of high school students attended for free. People still talk about it. I still think it's a great model.

In 1996, Biola paid to have Warren Duffy, host of the *Live from LA* show on the big Christian radio station 99.5 FM KKLA, come on campus to do his live, three-hour afternoon-drivetime show. In the agreement, Biola got three 15-minute segments, and Talbot was given one of them.

Dennis Dirks asked me to go on and talk about TIBS. The segment went well, and as soon as we went to break, the producer of the show, Duane Patterson, asked me if I'd like to guest-host for Duffy a few weeks later. I leaped at the opportunity.

I arrived at Duffy's studios a nervous wreck. I had been a guest on radio and television shows but had never carried a show on my own—let alone for three hours, and let alone on what's called a "hard clock." That means, because the show is networked, you have "hard breaks": You have to finish a segment exactly on time, or you're simply cut off. No such thing as running long. No such thing as a graceful exit if you misjudge your time. I was told that music would start in my earphones 45 seconds prior to the hard break. It would get progressively louder until the cutoff moment. That would give me warn-ing, and time, to organize my thoughts and segue to the break.

I gathered all my notes and braced for my first nine-minute seg-ment. I was more nervous than I ever was on the mound pitching to some Hall of Famer with the game on the line. The show got under way, and I started talking. You know how you can carry an internal conversation with yourself while you're talking aloud? On the out-side, I don't even remember what I was saying, but on the inside, my mind was thinking, "What's the matter with that red clock? Why's it going so slow? I've been on the air a lot longer than four minutes. I'm running out of things to say here, and I've got another five min-utes to go! Argghhh!"

Then I realized that it wasn't just five more minutes, of course. After the break I'd still have nearly *three more hours* of this torture! "How can anyone possibly do this?" I moaned to myself. My shirt was soaked, I had to go to the bathroom, and I felt as if I was going to throw up.

Somehow, however, I kept talking. Then, thankfully, I heard deliverance on the way: The music Duane had talked about was waft-ing ever so softly into my headphones. "Hallelujah!" my brain shouted. I did my "out" as Duane had taught me, and the instant I thought I could begin to relax, as the music was playing in the back-ground, I heard Duane's voice in the headphones.

"Well, Frankie," he said, "this is the most expensive 40 seconds of music KKLA has ever played. You went out a little early, buddy."

I died inside. I'd signed off nearly a full minute early—an eternity in radio, and it was time they could have sold to advertisers.

Duane's voice continued reassuringly in my ear. "Hey, don't worry, buddy. It can only get better . . . because it can't get any worse."

Thus began my guest-host radio career.

Actually, it did get better. I was asked back again and again, sitting in for Duffy more than a hundred times over the next seven years. Duane went with Hugh Hewitt to start his national radio show a few years later, and I guest-hosted on Hugh's show about 50 times.

But back to ministry at Biola.

With the ongoing success of TIBS and my growing radio experience, Dennis Dirks gave me the green light to pursue getting Talbot on the radio. I had developed a relationship with Ambassador Advertising, which handles a lot of the big Christian shows, and they loved the idea of addressing current news from a Christian worldview. They asked me to put together a demo for them.

We put a Talbot panel together and taped a couple of shows at Ambassador in January 1998. They were raw; I'd need experience running that model of program as opposed to guest-hosting someone else's show. But the core was there.

With Ambassador's encouragement, I raised the money to buy 13 weeks of broadcast time on a little station in Los Angeles. My assistant was Marty Russell, who helped me run the TIBS program and was also my producer for the Biola radio show. She and I remodeled the Biola radio studio ourselves. We bought the furniture, painted the walls, and even changed out the soundproofing, all on the TIBS budget. We would be on the air in about 4 weeks.

In February 1999, Biola president Clyde Cook invited me to dinner to bring him up to date on the latest developments. He congratulated me on my success thus far and assured me that since I had raised all the money and remodeled the studio at our own expense, costing the university nothing, I had total control of the radio show under Dennis Dirks's leadership. I shared with him the even better news that Ambassador had a million-dollar donor interested in funding Biola's return to national radio, once I had gained the necessary experience to run the Talbot-panel style show. He was thrilled.

Life was beautiful. We'd refine the model for 13 weeks and then put Talbot on national radio. TIBS was reaching about 300 adults a week in a dozen churches around LA. I was teaching another Biola undergraduate course in the apologetics department, in TIBS twice a week, hosting for Hugh and Duffy, and speaking at a lot of conferences and men's retreats.

My ministry had never been more effective. Gina was happy that our life had finally stabilized. We were no longer living on the little baseball savings we had left after our experience with the IRS. Our son, Frank, was 18 and in college. He was going to Biola at a reduced rate because I was on staff. Our daughter, Christina, was almost 15 and flourishing at the local Christian school. Our marriage was great. We loved our friends and enjoyed our times together. The bluebirds were singing.

Then the bluebirds hit the fan, and feathers flew everywhere.

30

★ ★ ★

GETTING JUMPED, PART TWO

There's no need for me to reveal names and sordid details about some of the people I worked with at Talbot and Biola long ago. The problems began like this: I was invited to a clandestine meeting by guys I loved and respected. They were plotting to overthrow Biola's president, Clyde Cook.

I left the meeting, came home, and told Gina I felt like I needed to take a bath.

"It's just dirty business," I told her, "and I thought this was ministry. But it's no better than the world. I've got to warn him."

"You can't," Gina told me. "If you do, they'll blackball you from ministry. You need these guys for almost everything, from TIBS to the radio show to teaching at Biola, all the conferences and retreats, everything."

"So what do I do?" I asked her.

"Don't say anything. Just tell them you don't want to go to the meetings anymore." Gina sighed. "But Frank," she continued, "they're going to blackball you anyway. With guys like this, you're either with them or against them."

"Well, I can't be with them," I said.

"Then you're gonna get blackballed," said Gina, who has the gift of prophecy.

"Oh no," I said. "They'll never do that. They're Christian leaders."

I got blackballed.

The biggest reason I had chosen to go to Talbot was to learn from these guys. I looked up to them. They were my mentors. We hung out together. Their opinions had become my own. I felt as if I was on the inside track. When they'd dish the dirt about other people and ministries, I got the scoop on a lot of big names in Christianity, people in leadership at Biola and Talbot, and a host of other apologetics ministries. I heard a lot of stuff I still wish I didn't know. Gradually I began to realize that they weren't the men of integrity I'd thought they were.

Now, their final loyalty test for me was whether I would join them in their coup against Clyde. When I declined, I got their passive wrath. Passive because I had dirt on them. Had it been the Mafia, they would have put a hit on me. I knew too much about some of their unethical activities—practices for which they would later be disciplined.

But this wasn't the Mafia. This was ministry. So they put a kinder, gentler hit on me—character assassination by slander and gossip. To my face they acted as though nothing had changed. But all the while, they were destroying my reputation.

A lot went on, too many events to recount here, events that some of the others involved might not see the same way I do. There were arguments, political dogfights, turf wars, and more. But as I said earlier, spilling all that now would only damage more reputations. I'm not interested in revenge.

Churches began canceling TIBS. Instructors were suddenly "unavailable" to teach. Conferences and retreats politely uninvited me. The phone stopped ringing for speaking requests. I wasn't asked to teach in the undergraduate program for the next semester. I started getting odd looks from faculty and staff. The million-dollar donor who'd wanted to fund our radio ministry suddenly evaporated.

And then, the big event . . .

I had appeared on Bill Maher's *Politically Incorrect* for a second time in October 1999 and had gotten into it with Bill's other guests, who were going after me for being a prolife, conservative Christian. It was good programming, the producers loved it, and I held my own in the four-on-one gang up that was the format of his show.

I got asked back. I thought it went well. Edgy, but well.

A few days later, on October 15, 1999, the vice president for university advancement at Biola called me into his office. I liked Wes Willmer—still do—but it was his responsibility to deliver the bad news. The decision had already been made. We were joined by two others, the provost and the dean of Talbot School of Theology.

"Frank, we're ending your radio show," Wes told me. "President Cook has received several complaints and one letter from a Christian leader. This leader was very critical of your appearance on *Politically Incorrect*. He said that you should not be representing an evangelical university, that it was conduct unbecoming of a Christian gentleman. So it's time for us to part ways."

My brain was working in slow motion. I was being let go. Fired.

"And Frank," Wes continued more gently, "your radio show is really not a very good fit for the university. The topics are too edgy. Many in our constituency will be upset with almost any issue you take on. We need to find a gracious way to close down the program. I think you have potential in radio, but not here."

I couldn't get past the screaming reality of the moment. Stunned, shocked, immobilized, I said the first thing that popped into my head.

"What about my son's Biola scholarship?" I asked.

"According to the university's human resources policy, the tuition remission ends with your employment. He'll be allowed to finish out this semester under scholarship, but beginning next semester, it will not be available," Wes said apologetically.

It was Pete Rose releasing me all over again.

I got up and walked out of Wes's office, went to my desk, and boxed up my stuff. Marty Russell, my assistant, was away from her desk since she and Gina were on campus having lunch. I called them and asked them to meet me in the parking lot.

They climbed into my car, worried looks on their faces. We drove around the block, off campus, because I needed a comfort cigar.

"You won't believe what just happened," I began. "They fired me. No more TIBS. No more radio show. No more teaching. Frankie's scholarship ends this semester; he'll have to go somewhere else next year. It's all gone."

Tears rolled down my cheeks, but I held it together for Gina and Marty.

After we got home, I went out to my backyard and watched the moon rise in the dark sky.

"God, what are You doing?" I screamed inside. "This is so wrong. I hate this! I work my butt off for You and create all this ministry out of nothing, run TIBS on my laptop, raise the money for the radio show, get all this publicity on national television for Biola, host these big shows here in LA, and this is what You do to me! Are You kidding me?

"I didn't get involved in the coup against the president, and now he fires me! These guys are slandering me all over the place, and I don't say squat about them, and they win and I lose? Are You up there or not?

"If this is ministry, You can have it. I don't want anything more to do with Your church, or any more of this Christian BS. It's over. You can have it. S— ministry!"

31

★ ★ ★

SITTING ON MY BUCKET

When my elbow got shattered and my baseball career eventually ended, it was painful. But when my ministry dream shattered, the pain went deeper. It was more like a death.

I stopped going to church. I didn't lose my faith in God; I knew He was there, but I was mad at Him and seriously disillusioned with His people. I felt as if they were all a bunch of Mafia crooks and that being in ministry was like dealing with the Corleone family. If you didn't do what these people wanted, they rubbed you out and you slept with the fishes, so to speak.

It wasn't as if I was without sin or fault. Obviously. But my heart was pure in the sense that I wasn't interested in the political maneuvering and power plays. I really just wanted to teach Christian worldview. I loved the ministry, and I loved seeing God change people's lives. As they learned the Bible and discovered more about the nature of God, they were influencing others in their offices, classrooms, and neighborhoods.

What really ticked me off about the way I was let go was the fakeness and betrayal of my so-called friends. In time I learned that the very people who were smiling at my face were the ones stabbing me in the back. All that took me back to my growing-up years and to what I had hated most.

When I was a kid, I never knew if my mom was lying or telling the truth. She lied about her past, lied about what she was doing in the present; and we lied too, keeping up appearances, acting as if we were a seminormal, happy family when we weren't.

As you know, I'd learned that the truth about anything was the opposite of whatever my mother told me. So, to take that small but bruising episode from my elementary-school years, when my mom had told me I was a great singer, I learned that the opposite was true when I launched into my infamous, horrific tryout rendition of "Born Free."

And of course my mother's biggest deception was that atheism was true and Christianity was stupid. So when I came to faith in Christ, I saw for the first time that truth really existed. I learned that truth was reliable, firm, and absolute. It could be trusted.

As I'd grown in my new faith, I knew that Christians, though saved, were imperfect. Just like me. But I also believed that Christians, particularly leaders in ministry, should be, for the most part, truth tellers. I believed that what they said could be trusted. And because I'd grown up in my mother's twisted world and had such a deep hatred for keeping up appearances, I detested facades. I hated hypocrisy. I couldn't stand it when people smiled and acted as if everything was great when it wasn't. It drove me nuts. Still does.

So when Biola ended the radio show, when I discovered that people had been hugging me in Christian love and then turning around and betraying me, I felt as if my guts had been ripped out.

Gina cried a lot during this period. But I didn't weep. I didn't yell. I just sat on my bucket in the backyard, teaching kids how to pitch. I smoked a lot of cigars, staring up at majestic Mount Baldy in the distance and at the dry, splintered wood of my backyard fence, right there behind my young pitchers. Maybe it was a metaphor: I knew I was going to be all right in the far distance of the long run, safe in heaven. But my immediate future wasn't so lovely. It looked as dry and broken as my splintered back fence.

I wasn't particularly in touch with my emotions, but I knew I was mad. Or disillusioned. Or some combination of the two.

S— ministry! I thought for the hundredth time. *Ministry is a total waste of time. I wasted a bunch of money on a useless degree chasing this stupid ministry dream, my son lost his free education, I put my family through all this poverty and heartache over the past 12 years—all for what? Now I don't have a real job, I'm not qualified to do anything, and no one will hire me. My family's hurting.*

What was the point? Where is God in all this? How can this possibly be redeemed? It's as if my life is in a thousand little pieces, like a big jigsaw puzzle without any picture on the cover of the box. I have no idea how to put the pieces together again.

Besides sitting on my bucket and teaching private pitching lessons, all I wanted was a new game. Or maybe to run away and open a bait shop or something; just get away from it all. Or maybe it was time to finally go to law school. I wasn't sure how to find it, but I just wanted a place where people were real, and I could just do my thing—whatever that was. But I knew it wasn't in ministry. No way. Never again!

I had been bucket sitting for a while when Gina got a call in November 1999 from our friend, my former assistant Marty Russell, inviting us over for dinner. Her husband, Walt, was a professor at Talbot, and someone I had grown to respect. He was a gentle man with a pastor's heart and a gift for mentoring leaders. We accepted their invitation for dinner with a few friends.

After the meal we gathered in the Russells' living room. Everyone was kicking around the idea of starting a small group together, and they all seemed gung ho about it. Gina was tired of watching me sit on the bucket coaching pitchers. She wanted to plug in to a group of people.

So everyone seemed to think that a small group would be a great idea. Except me. I had been pretty quiet and withdrawn during the meal, and by this time it was clear that one of the big purposes of the get-together was to get Frank to talk about what he was thinking and feeling.

But Frank was clammed up and shut down.

"So," said Walt jovially, "what do you think about joining our small group?"

"Well, I'm okay with it," I told him, "but don't expect me to contribute a whole bunch. I'm pretty much out of gas when it comes to God, ministry, and all that 'praise the Lord' stuff."

Marty asked, "How are you feeling now about what happened at Biola, Frank? It's been a few months."

"Oh, I'm fine," I lied. "I'm doing pitching lessons almost every day. It's paying the bills. I'm thinking of going to law school. In fact, I bought an LSAT prep book just a few days ago. I'm busy. I'm okay."

"But, Frank," Judy said, "that's not what Marty asked. She asked how you're feeling, not what you're thinking of doing." Judy TenElshof was a psychologist who taught at Talbot, and she and her husband, Gene, had known the Russells for years. I liked them a lot.

"Aren't you ticked off at Biola for what they did to you?" asked

Gene. "I remember when I got let go in corporate. I was furious. Come on, you can tell us. How are you really feeling about it?"

I then began to open up, just a little bit. But the more I talked, the more I sounded like a guy reporting on a movie he'd just watched rather than the guy who'd been sliced by the shards of his broken ministry dream. I wasn't in touch with my feelings at all. I was living out of my head, able to share information but unable to be real about my emotions because I didn't know what they were.

"You're splitting," Judy said. "You're stuffing your emotional pain and pretending it doesn't exist. You're not okay. We love you, and we think you ought to talk to someone about what's going on inside. We think you should go for some counseling. We know someone we think you should talk to."

I looked around. They were all nodding in agreement. My eyes locked with Gina's. I could tell she was hoping and praying that I'd say yes. Later she said that watching me sit on that bucket every day was like watching a man dying from emotional cancer, in denial the whole time.

We left the dinner party, and I thought about what Judy had said. Maybe some guys would have had a hard time going to a mental-health professional. I know it has a stigma in some circles, like if you're just spiritual enough, or man enough, you don't need counseling. Just stuff it down, keep a stiff upper lip. Act like it's okay, no matter what. I had done that my whole life.

I'd never thought about going to a psychologist or psychiatrist. As deranged as my mother was, it just wasn't something people in our family did. It was for crazy people, and we were "normal."

Right.

But as an athlete I knew the difference between working out by myself and working out with a professional trainer. It made sense to me that if I needed to get in better shape emotionally and spiritually, I should go to a professional. It seemed to me that most of us seek professional help in just about every area of life, from finances to legal issues to car maintenance to physical health, so why wouldn't I do the same in terms of my mental health?

Fortunately we were still on Major League Baseball™ insurance, and it would cover the counseling. So I made an appointment, got off my bucket, and walked into a therapist's office one fall morning in 1999.

Judy had recommended I see a woman about my age who had spent years on the mission field before returning to the United States to become a psychologist and professor. That's all I knew about her. I expected to meet a power player wearing a white coat, a professional analyst from Central Casting. Instead I was greeted by Dr. G, a gentle lady who looked as though she should have been wearing an apron and serving cookies to the neighborhood kids.

I was not impressed.

She is going to be my counselor? I thought.

Over the next year or so, Dr. G, would morph from a harmless-looking Yoda into a Master Jedi Knight against the forces of darkness that had been keeping me in bondage my entire life. But at that first meeting I was judging by appearances.

"Okay," I said, ready to take control and tell Dr. G exactly what she needed to know. My expert analysis could save us both a lot of time. "I'm 42 years old. I've been the nerdy geek, the high school sports star, the class president who dated the cute cheerleader, the

Major League™ player who was flying high, and the poor injured pitcher whose throwing arm was messed up.

"Then I became a Christian, went through a bunch of ministry false starts, and then became what I thought was a pretty decent trainer, teacher, and apologist for the faith. I was happy, fulfilled, thinking I was doing what God wanted me to do. Gina was happy. My kids were happy. Things were great.

"Then one day that picture-perfect life, and that man I see in the mirror every morning, got totally shattered, just like my baseball career. And now I don't know who I am, who I can trust, what I'm supposed to be doing, what God is up to, or where I go from here. All I know is that I'm mad as h—, and I don't know at who or why."

Dr. G's eyes filled with tears as she listened to my passionless executive summary of my life.

"Why are you crying and I'm not?" I asked when I had finished, proud of the fact I wasn't feeling anything.

"That's why you're here," she said.

Clearly Dr. G had her work cut out for her.

32

★ ★ ★

SHATTERED MIRRORS

At our next meeting, Dr. G began by asking me a really tough question:

"How are you feeling?"

I stared at her for a minute.

"Uh . . ." I said, going down my mental checklist, "the baseball tutoring is going great. I'm packed and can't accept any more students. I'm studying for the LSAT, and I've started running. I think I want to run a marathon. The kids are both doing great. Gina's fine. And I've lost a few pounds. Things are good."

Dr. G listened kindly.

"No," she said. "I asked you how you're *feeling*."

"You know, Judy asked me that too. I guess I don't know what you mean," I said honestly. "What kind of answer are you looking for?"

"Tell me about your emotions, what you're feeling inside," she led.

"I honestly don't know how to answer that question. When you ask about feelings, I reach down into that box, and I can't find anything. It's like asking me, 'How tall is purple?' I don't even know what an answer looks like. What words do I use?"

Dr. G got up and went over to her desk. She pulled out a chart and brought it back to me. It looked as if it had been designed for small children, like those visual aids hospitals use to get kids to tell doctors their degree of pain. It had little faces with various expressions, and next to the faces were words. Excited. Joyful. Hopeful. Sad. Afraid. Frustrated. Gloomy. Anxious. Nervous. And so forth.

I stared at the chart and its little emoticons. I didn't know much about emotions, I guess. So if Dr. G, or anybody else, asked me how I was feeling, I could only respond with what I was thinking. Evidently I'd blocked my feelings for a long time. Evidently my mother had something to do with that.

Dr. G and I met for weeks that turned into months. It would be both impossible and a bit self-indulgent to try to recapture our discussions for this book. All you need to know are some of the ways I learned a few good things. I began to have little breakthroughs; I began to think and feel in a different way. Dr. G would pick up on seemingly random pieces of my life and lead me to connect the dots. In counseling terms, I began to become more integrated—rather than fragmented—as a person.

Around the time I realized I couldn't express how I was feeling without my remedial emoticon chart, I discovered that I'd stuffed my emotions for years. Sure, I'd been happy, and sad, and mad; I wasn't a robot.

But before I came to faith in Christ, I'd suppressed emotions because many of them were too painful to acknowledge. And then after I began believing in God, I suppressed many emotions for a different reason: I thought some of them were wrong, sinful, or just bad, that I *shouldn't* be feeling certain ways.

"Good Christians shouldn't feel this way," I'd tell myself, and I'd slam the door to that emotion. More closed doors in my heart. I had embraced a Christianity of the mind, but I hadn't let Jesus become the Lord of my heart. I didn't know how.

Now, from Dr. G I began to learn that emotions weren't right or wrong. They weren't good or bad or true or false. They were simply feelings. The key is rooting out their source. Once you do that, you can then identify both what you're feeling and why you're feeling it. Or, in my case, what I *wasn't* feeling.

Dr. G was also a master, as I've said, at helping me connect the dots in my life. I told her silly stories from my childhood, things that seemed utterly superficial, but for some reason they'd lodged in my memory. For example, I told Dr. G how my dad was always casual—a cigar clenched between his teeth, wearing Ray-Ban sunglasses, work boots, khaki pants, and work shirts.

Dr. G looked back at me, raising an eyebrow. "You mean pretty much exactly like how you look right now?"

I took stock. My Ray-Bans were in my pocket, I had an unlit cigar in my mouth, and I was wearing a work shirt, jeans, and boots. I wondered how long it would have taken me to notice this on my own: I wanted to look like my dad. We explored why that was, after all those years of totally negative input about my dad, courtesy of my mother.

Another time, after I'd been seeing Dr. G for a while, I told her about Christmas when I was seven years old. I had really, really, really wanted a purple Sting-Ray bike. Miracle of miracles, my parents had gotten it for me. It sat in all its glory next to the Christmas tree. The next day I rode it to the mall, where it was promptly stolen.

Dr. G knew my favorite pastime was riding the tricked-out motorcycle I had bought after I'd begun to experience some real changes through therapy. She knew that I babied my big Honda VTX.

"Frank," she asked, "what color is your motorcycle?"

Ding! The bell rang, the lights went on, and the dots came together.

"Purple," I told her. "Just like my Sting-Ray. I guess I found my bike after all, didn't I?"

Connecting my childhood to my adulthood may not seem like a big deal. But there was great healing in it. As I began to realize how I'd unconsciously honored my dad by dressing like him, it was of course in direct response to the way my mom had constantly devalued him. I began to experience a huge, gaping sense of loss that was much bigger than the loss of a purple Sting-Ray as a kid. I began to feel anger, deep anger, against my mother because she'd robbed me so completely of what I could have had with my dad. Why was she so malicious? Why would a woman do that? In fact, come to think of it, why would a mother leave a little four-year-old boy alone? Why was I a latchkey kid as a *preschooler*?

Then I would get analytical. Well, my mother was mentally ill. She didn't know any better. It wasn't her fault. She was a victim too.

At this point Dr. G entered in, very gently. "Frank, your mother may have had issues. But she was responsible. What she did was *wrong*. Moms don't leave four-year-olds alone!"

I stared at her.

Then tears started sliding out of Dr. G's eyes.

I stared at her some more. What was wrong?

"Am I missing something?" I asked.

"Frank!" Dr. G exclaimed. "This is so *sad*! You're not feeling it, but it's so very sad!"

As time went on with Dr. G, my analytical brain and my wounded heart began to connect. I'd be telling Dr. G some story and begin to bawl. As they say, I got in touch with my feelings in a big way. And that's a good thing.

The main thing I learned from Dr. G had to do with mirrors. I'm not big on psychological buzzwords, but this concept made a lot of sense to me at the time, and it still does today. It's pretty obvious. We all look to the people around us for a reflection, or feedback, of who we are. Children get this sense of self from their parents. If you're told as a child that you're loved, that you're smart, that you can achieve great things, then that's how you tend to think of yourself. If you're told that you're a worthless piece of crap, then your self-image isn't likely to be so good. A false mirror gives you a false picture of yourself. An accurate mirror shows who you are, warts and all.

My mother was a horribly distorted mirror. Because of her chronic lies, my early view of myself was seriously skewed. I was whatever my mom's fake fantasy of the day made me. So one day she might tell me I was a great singer, when I really wasn't. One day she might tell me that I looked great, when in reality I had 21 cavities, never brushed my teeth, and was as soft as a Krispy Kreme doughnut. One day she might tell me I was the victim of all those other kids who were jealous of me because I was a genius. And of course every day she'd tell me that I was an atheist, because God didn't exist.

I shook off this thinking in stages. In one meeting with Dr. G, I recalled when I first began to make the break from Mom's skewed views. I was a sophomore in high school. I was in the backyard, and my mom had just gotten off the phone with my half sister, Lynn, whom I'd seen maybe six times in my entire life.

Mom wanted me to do something for Lynn, and all of a sudden I just burst out, "Why? I don't even know her! She's not my sister! No!"

My mother grabbed a rake that was lying nearby and swung it at me with all her might. I turned at the last second of her swing. The rake's claws just missed my head; the handle broke across my back.

I stared at my mom. She had never hit me before. She never lost control. But now her face was twisted with rage: "Of course you'll do what I'm telling you to do! How dare you challenge me? I've given you everything you have; I've made you who you are. You ungrateful little bastard; you're just like your father!"

I brushed the splintered wood off my shoulder and left the backyard. It was a turning point. I finally clearly understood that my mom's reflection of reality couldn't be trusted.

Meanwhile, I didn't really have much of a sense of identity that came from my dad. When I was little, we played catch and he was my hero, but as I got older, my dad was strangely absent. He was there, but he wasn't much of an influence. I didn't look to him for who I was or what I could do. He wasn't a good mirror either.

When I was older, like most teenagers, I looked to my friends for identity. I became whatever other kids told me was cool. A good ballplayer, a funny guy, a trendsetter. During sophomore year of high school, Mr. Steck entered my life. Because of his encouragement, I learned I had a mind. I began to grow into an adult. He was my first decent mirror.

Then, in Gina's eyes, I saw the strong, good man she believed me to be—the man I wanted to become.

Eventually, as I came to believe in God, I saw myself as His son. As I studied the Bible, I learned that my worth wasn't about *what I did* but *who I was* in Christ. I knew theologically that I was beloved of God, bought at an incredible price, imbued by Him with gifts and abilities for His service. I knew lots of stuff in my head about a healthy identity in Christ. I just didn't have one.

I was like an anorexic woman who always sees herself 30 pounds overweight. My sense of identity was based on inaccurate perceptions. I became whoever I thought people wanted me to be. I was a people pleaser on steroids. I was constantly searching for new mirrors, and along the way, images from the bad ones kept popping into my head.

My family mirror had shattered. My baseball mirror had shattered. And now, my ministry mirror had shattered as well.

I wasn't sure I could ever put my Humpty Dumpty self back together again . . . because I'd never been "together" in the first place.

33

★ ★ ★

GETTING RECYCLED

I was in weekly therapy with Dr. G for about nine months, from late 1999 to June 2000. Almost every week I had one of those "Aha!" moments, where I saw the connections between my dysfunctional childhood and my attitudes and behaviors in the present. It was like opening gifts that had been lost in the attic. I loved counseling. I couldn't get over the fact that God, through Dr. G, was showing me wounds that had been hidden for so long—and healing them.

It was painful, though. Many nights I would wake to Gina's soft hand on my shoulder, letting me know that my sobbing had woken her up . . . again.

Dr. G was giving me a new way of seeing, a new mirror, one that in time would more accurately reflect reality, one that would show my wounds and scars, God's healing, and my gifts and strengths. Slowly the image of the man I would become began to form.

I began to see reasons for habits I'd had all my life. My inability to sustain close friendships was rooted in the fact I'd always been the new kid in school. The awkwardness (that no one else would have seen) that I felt in group settings—whether a locker room, Thanksgiving dinner, or just hanging out with friends—was rooted in my "new kid" need to perform. I often withdrew from people because I'd never had a family in which it was okay to just "be." I always had to *do* things to prove myself. I saw that my tendency to seek solitude had sometimes isolated me from Gina and our kids, and it was rooted in being an only child with no friends, no extended family, and anti-social parents who never entertained guests.

There were so many things about me that I just didn't like. Sometimes I got impatient with my slow rate of progress. Dr. G helped me not to be too hard on myself, to realize God's patient, healing hand. Over time I began to see that God could redeem—and use for good—even the harmful, hurtful pieces of my past.

Gina and the kids began noticing little differences. I became more emotionally present. I could empathize and sympathize more easily. I listened better and asked open-ended questions rather than just offering quick practical solutions from on high, which comes naturally to most dads. The kids and I had longer conversations. They opened up more and more as they saw that I was really interested in their thoughts and feelings. Gina and I reached a much deeper level of intimacy, talking for hours, laughing, crying, really connecting. It was exhilarating, liberating, and just plain fun.

It was as though I'd been using a small box of emotional crayons all my life, in just the primary colors. Now I had a big palette of oils. If my pre-Christian experience had been life in black and white, and my early Christian life in a few colors, now I was living in high density. My breakthrough in therapy made me want to do something to mark the new me. Something fun, daring, and dangerous. I had always wanted a motorcycle, but while I was a baseball player, I didn't think it was worth the risk. After baseball, with our financial problems, I just couldn't afford it. Plus, my kids were too little.

But the time had come, I thought, to unleash my inner biker.

Gina wasn't too keen on the idea. I could have tried to rational-
ize it to her with something like "Christina has her driver's permit
now, so we're going to need another set of wheels, and a bike for me
is cheaper than a car," but that would have been a lie. I wanted a
motorcycle, and that was that.

I took out some extra life insurance and headed to the dealer, and
as I mentioned earlier, bought a purple motorcycle. I knew I'd like
having a bike, but I had no idea how much I'd love it. Gina rides with
me, but only under pretty specific conditions: It's got to be between 76
and 84 degrees, daylight, no rain, and preferably in Yosemite, Tahoe,
Mammoth, or just around the neighborhood. No busy streets, high-
ways, or freeways. And only for about two hours max.

I, on the other hand, have logged more than 160,000 miles on my
bike—in snow, sleet, rain, hail, and a scorching 120 degrees in
Phoenix. I dream one day of doing an Iron Butt Four Corners Tour,
hitting all four corners of the continental United States in three weeks.

I can't help but notice that most of the megachurch pastors I
know—at least in Southern California—also ride. So do a significant
number of heads of Christian organizations, come to think of it.
Maybe there's some connection between ministry, stress, and the joy
of hitting the open road on your Harley. That's why God invented
motorcycles.

One time I was riding outside Lake Tahoe. It was a perfect day. I
was listening to Bad Company on my iPod, tooling along at about
6,000 feet, loving life. The only problem was that the altitude kept
plugging my ears. I was yawning to get them to pop and holding my
nose and blowing out. But that wasn't working, and I really didn't
want to have to stop, take off my helmet, take out my earbuds, and
jump up and down trying to get my ears unplugged.

The last thing I remember was thinking, "I'll just try to hold my nose and blow out one more time . . ."

Next thing I knew I was lying flat on my back, dreamily gazing up at the clear blue sky. A guy I'd never seen before was leaning over me.

"You okay, buddy?" he asked. "You okay?"

Never been better, I thought. *This is so nice.*

Then it began to dawn on me that I was lying in the middle of the road. I began running through a mental checklist of my body parts. Can I wiggle my toes? Check. Legs? Check. Arms? Check. Am I all here? Check.

Slowly I became aware of an intense pain in my right heel. I inched my head up: Ah, look, there was my 700-pound motorcycle resting directly on my foot. Then I realized my left shoulder was ripped up, my left wrist was damaged, my left hip hurt . . . yeah, I must've had a wreck.

I had no idea if I'd been lying in the road for two minutes or two hours. My guardian angel was right there, though, still asking if I was okay.

"Yeah," I said weakly, "but can we get this motorcycle off my foot?"

He pulled the cycle off my heel. He'd already somehow taken off my helmet and put it neatly with my backpack, iPod, and a few other personal items he must have gathered off the road. There was a huge gash in my helmet, the shifting mechanism had been sheered off my bike, and the mirror was snapped off.

My guardian angel was tall and thin, with dark hair and eyes. "Can I call anybody for you?" he asked.

"No, no, I'm okay," I said.

I somehow got my stuff together, got back on the bike, and rode down the mountain in third gear. The guy followed me in his truck until I got to town . . . and then he disappeared. I never even got to tell him good-bye.

Obviously I could have been killed several times over in this little incident. I told friends about it the next day and found out that in trying to pop my ears I'd created a "vagal response," the temporary cessation of oxygen to the brain that caused me to pass out and my bike to spin out. So I haven't popped my ears since, and all is well.

34

★ ★ ★

A DIVINE CONSPIRACY

Cycling adventures aside, after nine months of counseling with Dr. G, I decided to stop our sessions. As I was getting healthier, I didn't want to go any further without Gina coming along on the adventure. It was like setting sail to an exotic isle, and you don't want to leave your lover on the dock. I wanted Gina to come with me to a new way of thinking, communicating, and being.

Gina and I met with Dr. G together once, and then Gina started going on her own. Our marriage seemed to get better and better. The silly fights that had plagued us since eloping 22 years earlier were getting fewer and fewer. We realized that we had both fallen into the unhealthy patterns of conflict resolution that had been modeled for us by our parents. So my way of dealing with conflict was to pretend it wasn't happening, and Gina's was to yell and throw dishes.

We began learning new communication skills not only with each other but also with our kids. We always had a good marriage, but now we were creating a great marriage, piece by piece. It wasn't as if we were sailing off into a perfect sunset, happily ever after. But the fact was, we were in the same boat, of the same mind, and we were happy together. We were facing whatever lay ahead with the sense that our past didn't have to dictate our future.

Through Dr. G and a new sense of God's grace, I was seeing beyond the hurt of what had happened at Talbot. I'd seen that God was still God, and there was real hope, even when Christians acted like idiots. And oddly enough, I still wanted to work one day in Christian radio. I was guest-hosting for Warren Duffy about twice a month on KKLA, and down deep, I knew I'd love a show of my own. But I couldn't imagine that happening. In terms of employment I was still wandering in the wilderness.

My main spiritual food during this time in the desert came through the ministry of Dallas Willard. For some unknown reason I had decided to run a marathon, and I'd listen to Dallas's tapes while I ran. Later I'd listen to them again, take notes on my laptop, and paraphrase what he was saying so that I could own it. Willard's *The Divine Conspiracy* is the most meaningful book I've ever read. I put together a study guide for it and used it to teach in local churches and at conferences. Even now, hardly a day goes by when I don't have at least one thought rooted in something I learned from God while reading *The Divine Conspiracy*. If I was marooned on a desert island, I'd want the Bible and *The Divine Conspiracy*.

Okay, so I really love that book. A gigantic paradigm shift occurred in my thinking as a result of it. So much emphasis in popular Christian literature is focused on dealing with your personal sin, your personal fulfillment, and God's will for your life. These are of course crucial issues, but they tend to pull one's focus toward oneself.

All of us want to live for something bigger than ourselves. We want to be part of a Big Story. We want a cause, a purpose, for which we are willing to die. The gospel is about far more than just me and my life. It's majestic, magnificent—the victory of good over evil. Jesus won the *ultimate* war over evil by His death and resurrection, but we can participate with Him in the spiritual battles that still rage here on earth, seeking to overcome evil in all its forms.

When we Christians huddle in our churches, afraid of the world, we've lost the passion that compelled the great saints of the past. God loved the world enough to redeem it, and He calls us to take part in His redemption. He motivates us to hate injustice, to love mercy, to preach the good news to the poor just as Jesus did. If we are indifferent to evil, we won't confront it, and if we don't confront it, we can't defeat it. God calls us to go boldly out to the field of battle, to touch wounded lives, to march against an enemy whose defenses cannot prevail against us.

That's the kind of vision that gets me up every morning!

And it's the vision that eventually got me off my backyard bucket. I was still coaching pitching students, but something was changing. Then I received a phone call that didn't seem particularly significant. But now, looking back, it was another stepping-stone for God to lead me out of the wilderness of my frustration and pain.

35

★ ★ ★

FROM BUCKET
TO BROADCASTING

One spring day in 2001 I got a call from Pastor Chuck Smith of Calvary Chapel Costa Mesa. Pastor Chuck is legendary in Southern California as the leader God used to disciple young men who came to Christ during the Jesus movement of the '70s. A number of these guys, like Greg Laurie, in turn became pastors and evangelists who've led hundreds of thousands of people to Christ over the years.

Pastor Chuck asked me to meet with an ex-ballplayer, Dan Naulty, who had pitched a few years in the big leagues, most recently with the Yankees. Dan wanted to give pitching lessons and baseball clinics near the Calvary Chapel property in Costa Mesa. He wanted to use his sports platform to reach others for Christ, something I'd been doing for the past 15 years.

We met, and he laid out his plans. I'd done a bunch of camps and clinics and had even looked into opening a batting cage, but it never penciled out, primarily because of the high cost of liability insurance. So I was a bucket of cold water in Dan's face. I knew he was disappointed, but I didn't want him to make the mistake of thinking that because it was "ministry," it would somehow work. He could only lose money. I told him not to do it.

"But I want to do ministry," he said.

"What kind of ministry?" I asked.

"Well, if I can't do sports ministry, I want to teach. I want to go to seminary, get a master's degree, and teach somewhere," he said.

"But, Dan," I told him, "a master's degree ain't gonna cut it. The right way to do this, if you want to spend the rest of your life doing it, is to get a doctorate from a reputable school. I'm afraid you're going to spend a lot of your baseball money chasing this dream, and I don't want you to end up where I'm at."

"Frank," he said, "you've already gone to seminary, you've been teaching at all these places, doing conferences and retreats, you're on the radio guest-hosting . . . You've been doing what I would love to do!"

"No, Dan," I said. "Believe me, I'm not where you want to be. I can barely make a living doing this. If I wasn't going to be collecting my baseball retirement next year, I'd be off getting a PhD somewhere because I love teaching too. My master's degree qualifies me to teach high school, which is like perpetual AAA. Go for the big leagues! You gotta get the entrance card, which is a PhD. Don't settle for a master's. If you really want to teach, go get a doctorate as soon as you can!"

When I got home and told Gina about our conversation, another one of those connect-the-dots moments happened. Here I was giving Dan ministry counsel on what to do with his life now that his baseball career was over, and I wasn't even implementing my own advice. The fact was, if I really wanted to teach, I'd need a PhD too.

I thought back to the lunch I'd had a year earlier, in January 2000, with Dr. Larry Arnn, then president of the Claremont Institute. A mutual friend, Mike Morrell, had gotten us together to brainstorm about possible speaking events. The idea was that we'd do some cross-pollination. Larry would encourage Christians to care more about conservative politics, and I would encourage political conservatives to care more about the Christian worldview. This was our first get-together, just the three of us over lunch. In hindsight, I refer to what happened as my "political testimony."

I started the conversation after the initial round of small talk.

"Larry, I'm an evangelical, and I think we need to help people—conservatives, especially—understand the biblical foundation of our nation. The only real way to turn America around is to get Christians to be serious about walking with the Lord. We've simply moved too far away from our Christian roots. That's the whole problem."

"Frank, I'm a Christian too," Larry began. "But if—as you believe—all the answers are in the New Testament teachings of Jesus, then why do you think it took 18 centuries for there to be an America? Why would Christians want to create a new government when both the Lord and the book of Romans teach that we are to obey whoever is in power, even tyrants?

"Furthermore," he continued, "how would Christians, from the Bible alone, know how to even do such a thing? After all, Jesus never raised an army, levied a tax, guided a policy debate in a legislature, or administered a government."

I was stunned. Almost speechless. After an awkward silence I told him, "Larry, I'm embarrassed to say I've never even considered any of those questions. I don't have a clue as to how to answer, but I'm listening."

For the next two hours, Dr. Arnn laid out the broad contours of an answer. I had never heard anything like it. It was the story of political philosophy, the story of Christianity, the story of Western civilization, and the story of the American founding all rolled into one. He ranged with familiar ease from Plato's *Republic* to *The Federalist Papers*, with stops along the way to consider Jesus, the apostle Paul, Saint Augustine, Thomas Aquinas, Machiavelli, John Locke, Montesquieu, Thomas Jefferson, Abraham Lincoln, Winston Churchill, and Ronald Reagan, often quoting from memory.

I was blown away.

"Why have I never heard any of this before?" I asked him. "And if I haven't heard it—and I've been an adjunct professor at a Christian college—I guarantee you there's not one Christian in 100 who knows how to integrate Christianity with political philosophy. This is awesome! People need to hear this! I want to learn it; where do I start?"

"Well," he said, smiling a little at my enthusiasm, "Mike tells me you've talked about going to law school. I can tell you, you won't learn any of this at law school."

"Okay, then where? How? When?" I asked.

"At Claremont. If you're serious, and if you're man enough, you'll come do a PhD," he said.

"I don't have any money to do that," I told him.

"Let's take this one step at a time. Take the GRE and apply, and let's see what happens," Larry said.

And thus began my path to the PhD program in political philosophy and American government at Claremont Graduate University. I earned a half scholarship from CGU, and the other half of my tuition was picked up by the Salvatori Center under the direction of Charles Kesler, a friend of Larry's, and one of my favorite grad-school professors.

But, back to why I had never heard any of the information Larry shared. The short answer is because most schools and churches just don't teach it anymore. It's our lost history. It really isn't so much that Americans have lost their Christian roots, as you often hear. The fact is, Christians have lost their American roots. They don't really know that the American story and the larger story of Western civilization of which it is a part spring from *their* story. Given that ignorance, no wonder a shocking number of Christians today don't even register to vote. They don't understand that America was and is the greatest political expression of Christian values in history. Or, put another way, they don't understand that politics is theology applied. It's how we collectively live out our faith and love our neighbors as ourselves. Christian principles are good public policy.

Given my passion for these ideas, you can imagine that my three years in graduate school at Claremont flew by. I was chewing up the great ideas of Western civilization, digesting the principles that guided our nation's beginnings and mourning their erosion in today's increasingly secular, materialistic, naturalistic culture. I was engaged in a grand picture of life, culture, and the gospel. I was overflowing . . . and so it was providential that God continued to provide me with opportunities to guest-host frequently for Warren Duffy on KKLA, and to sit in for Hugh Hewitt on his national talk show.

When Duffy announced that he would be retiring at the end of 2003 after 10 years of hosting the afternoon drive-time show in LA, I put my name in for consideration to take his place. I knew that actually getting the LA show as a rookie would be like making the big leagues out of high school. It happens, but it's rare. There were so many talented, experienced conservative radio hosts across the country. I knew that if God was calling me to radio, I'd probably have to start in the minor leagues somewhere in the Midwest. Then maybe when I had more experience, I'd have a shot at the majors in Los Angeles or New York.

As I entered my final semester at Claremont, I was taking a full load of courses, in class three nights a week, each class with an intense reading list, weekly papers, a 20-pager due at the end of the semester, and, of course, final exams looming in December. Meanwhile I was guest-hosting regularly for Duffy and Hugh, speaking on the weekends, conducting private pitching lessons on Saturday and Sunday afternoons for spending money, and trying to be a good husband and father. In the near distance were the comprehensive qualifying exams for my PhD in the spring, followed by a dissertation.

One fall evening, as I was studying at my desk, I suddenly felt clammy and light-headed. My heart made a couple of flip-flops, and then I felt an electrical jolt in my left chest, similar to the jolt you get when you lick the terminals of a 9-volt battery. I yelled for Gina. My pulse was in the '40s. When we got to the hospital, I told them I was experiencing chest pain, and they rushed me right in. The cardiologist scheduled an immediate angiogram. No blockages, no evidence of anything amiss. I was going to make it, but they kept me overnight in the cardiac ICU just in case. In the end they attributed it to—yep, you guessed it—*stress*. Right. My life at that point was nothing but stress.

Two weeks later, Terry Fahy, the vice president of Salem Communications in Los Angeles, the guy who ran KKLA, called me to say they had narrowed the pool down to the final candidates. I was one of them. Was I free to come in and do a week of shows as a final audition?

Yes, I was. I pushed all the schoolwork aside for a week, and though I tried to keep up as best as I could, I of course fell behind in reading, papers, studying for exams . . . everything.

My audition week at KKLA went about as well as could be expected from a caffeine-overloaded, sleep-deprived, distracted PhD candidate with stress-induced heart palpitations.

A month went by. Then Terry called to invite me to a little meeting at the KKLA offices. They offered me the job: the 4:00 to 7:00 afternoon drive-time show, live, with call-ins about the hot political issues of the day. *The Frank Pastore Show* was an opportunity to do exactly what I loved to do most: talk, teach, and connect with people. I was beside myself with joy. And caffeine.

Leading up to my first week on the air, I had the dubious notion that I would somehow be able to prepare for the issues of a three-hour live show every day, do the show, drive an hour home, work on my dissertation for a few hours, sleep for about four hours, and get up the next morning and do it all over again. Weekends would be for library research and writing.

That fantasy didn't last long.

The following week I met with Charles Kesler. I needed to tell him I wouldn't be able to write a dissertation, and that I was deeply sorry for my inability to fulfill my commitment to the donors who had made my scholarship possible. It looked as if they had wasted their investment in me.

I will never forget the moment. It was as if God was showing me, once and for all, that I didn't have to be perfect for His grace to flow on me and through me. Charles listened patiently to my description of my situation, my apologies that I wasn't superhuman, and my sad assumption that he would hate me forever.

"Frank!" he said. "This is no waste of investment. We have lots of PhDs, but we don't have a whole lot of radio hosts. Go make us proud!"

36

★ ★ ★

FUN, FAST, AND REAL

Though I finished at Claremont with a master's degree in political philosophy and American government, rather than a PhD, my studies prepared me precisely for my work at KKLA. Early on we called *The Frank Pastore Show* "the intersection of faith and reason," and soon the whole station took on that brand. The idea came from my love of Thomas Aquinas, who in the 13th century took Augustine's theology and Aristotle's philosophy and integrated them as a way of looking at life that made reasonable sense, even to a nonbeliever.

I was no Aquinas, but I knew that many unbelieving people think of Christians as antiscientific idiots. That had been my view before my conversion. So I wanted to show listeners that science—good *unbiased* science—is not antifaith. Thinking Christians can be quite comfortable in the arenas of science, history, philosophy, government, and the issues of the day, because a Christian worldview is grand, bold, and extensive enough to inform these issues with real wisdom.

As I got rolling at KKLA, I felt I was doing the work that God had designed me to do. The show had, and has, plenty of gaffes and blunders; live radio is an imperfect science. But it's fun. It's fast. It's

real. And I love it. I try to keep my listeners surprised, engaged, hear-
ing ideas and insights they won't hear anywhere else. And so far, it
seems to be working.

But I hold it loosely.

Don't get me wrong: I'm fully invested in what I do. I give it my
all to make every show the best it can be. I work as hard as I can "as
unto the Lord," as the Bible puts it. But it's not like when I was "Frank
Pastore, pitcher"; take away the pitching, and I didn't know who I
was. Today I may be "Frank Pastore, radio host," but who I am, at the
deepest level, isn't dependent on my job, my ratings, or my fan mail.
I believe God has called me to this work, that it's ministry in that it
equips people to think with a Christian worldview—and that's good.
Very good. But my identity isn't tied up in my work. My identity is
tied up in God.

With live radio you can't pretend to be somebody you're not.
You've got to be real; you've got to set an emotional tone you can
deliver every day. I'm sure other radio hosts would make other com-
parisons, but for me, it's a lot like pitching. As soon as the red light
flashes on in the studio, it's like walking out to the mound. It's game
ON, and you've got to be consistent from your first pitch on the air
to your last pitch. With drive-time radio I've got to be as consistent
and pumped for the guy who tunes in at 6:45 PM as I was for the person who started listening to me at 4:00 PM. You can lose the game on
the first pitch or the last one. There's no such thing as a throwaway
segment, any more than a throwaway pitch.

Also like baseball, I know it's not all about me. A whole team
puts on the show, and I have no illusions, just as when I was pitching, that I'm irreplaceable. Sometimes, just like in pro sports, people
who happen to be in the spotlight on radio or TV can start thinking

it's all about them. When that happens on the air—particularly in a Christian context—it's pretty pitiful.

When I was playing ball, if I threw a bad pitch, I couldn't let it throw me. Same with radio. My show is divided into a series of nine- or ten-minute segments. Some are on current events, with me interviewing experts on the phone. Some are live call-ins, which our staff screen and prepare for the air. But with live radio you're always a few seconds away from disaster, and believe me, there's no do-over.

I have a little button on my control board that I can push when I need to cough, but there's no button that erases hundreds of thousands of listeners' memories if I say something really stupid. So it's risky. But if a segment crashes and burns, I can't let it shake me. It's like a bad pitch. You shake it off, thank God for commercials, and then, when the red light flashes on again, you throw your next pitch as well and as hard as you can.

Radio may be a somewhat solitary sport, trapped as one is in a glass-enclosed studio, but I've gained a strong sense of community from it. I love our audience. I don't know every person who listens, of course, but I know from e-mails, call-ins, and comments that people are on board with the show. It makes them think, laugh, and cry occasionally. It touches their lives.

It would be pretty stress inducing if it wasn't so fun. I sit in my studio every weekday, consuming enormous coffees with about four shots of espresso, courtesy of my friend Viktor, who owns the deli in our building. I've got my electronic toys set up all around me, Fox News scrolling the day's headlines, computer monitors available for me to Google anything in a second, call lines coming in, and my research on the topics of the day. I've got great people who come on regularly to discuss the issues of the day, such as Chuck Colson, David

Barton, Tony Perkins, Rick Warren, Joni Eareckson Tada, Ken Ulmer, Jay Richards, Francis Chan, John Townsend, Sean McDowell, and Hugh Ross, to name a few. My pastor, David Rosales, comes on the air to teach and pray for people when something particularly painful happens, like a mass shooting or some other type of loss. And I'm pushing the buttons, connecting with people, quaffing coffee, incredibly wired yet fully at ease, wearing a Hawaiian shirt, jeans, and cowboy boots.

Life is good.

It was a little odd the first time I guest-hosted for Dr. James Dobson at Focus on the Family. I walked into Dobson's studio in my usual attire, grinning big because I like Dr. Dobson so much, my shaved head gleaming. I was thrilled with the honor of being on the air at Focus.

"Well, Frank!" said Dr. Dobson, smiling at me. "I guess no one told you about our dress code here."

I dimly remembered that someone had said that men at the Focus offices are to wear coat and tie at all times. Evidently I had repressed that information because it was so unpleasant.

"So, Frank," Dr. Dobson continued, laughing and looking over my big flowered shirt, jeans, and boots. "What style do you call this, really? Are you, like, one of those metrosexuals, or what?"

Early on at KKLA, I introduced "Frank's Freaky Fridays," in which the last segment of the show was for call-ins. On some Freaky Fridays, for example, my guest was Dr. Heidi Sierra, who took calls from loopy people out there in Radio Land. Dr. Sierra was pretty loopy herself—she was a pet psychologist and animal astrologist. Callers could put their pet on the live phone line to connect with Dr. Sierra.

So, for example, Dr. Sierra took a query from a male caller—
Ted—who told her his dog, Barney, was exhibiting signs of anxiety
and depression.

"I don't know what's wrong with him, Doctor," said Ted.

"Could you just put him on the line, please?" said Dr. Sierra.

We could hear Ted whistling for Barney. "Here, boy! Come on!"

Then there was a slobber, and Barney got on the phone. "Woof,"
he said.

"Ah," said Dr. Sierra brightly. "Ted, what is Barney's astrological
sign?"

"Uh . . . I don't know," mumbled Ted.

"You care about this animal, but you haven't had his chart done?"
Dr. Sierra asked in disbelief.

Silence from Ted.

"Well," Dr. Sierra continued, "I know what Barney is trying to
tell me. You remember when you took care of your neighbor's
Pekingese last week?"

"Yes," Ted said sadly.

"Barney is trying to tell you, through his behavior, that he was
just really hurt when you had that other dog in the house."

"What do you recommend?" Ted asked.

"Well, counseling, of course," said Dr. Sierra. "And then some
aromatherapy and other organic interventions."

What listeners didn't realize at first was that Dr. Sierra, caller
Ted, and dog Barney were all actors, and that the whole thing was a
spoof. We did all kinds of variations of this type of thing on "Frank's
Freaky Fridays"—including Foil, a plant lover and liberationist who
married the ficus tree he rescued from Wal-Mart.

Listeners who caught on loved it. Those who didn't get it, how-

ever, couldn't understand why I was
plant liberationists on the air. We got wo
minded brethren might object to Freaky Friday
and now our Fridays are just as serious as every other

Sigh.

featuring dog astrologists and
ried that our more literal-
So we pulled them,
day of the week.

205

AND
AINS

I about forgiveness and ~~~~ ~~~~ of Christ, I began to learn about forgiveness and ~~~~~~~~~~n. These weren't familiar concepts for a young atheist.

The main person from whom I was estranged, of course, was my mother. As you know, around the time Gina and I eloped, I reluctantly helped my mom get her hooks back into my father after her relationship with Dude failed. She and my dad lived together in an apartment in Upland until he died in 1996.

I don't know how he stood it. My mother let herself go completely. She sprawled in a recliner most of the time, smoking and eating. She weighed about 300 pounds, and her hygiene habits, which were never much, actually got worse. She became the extended edition of herself, uncut, raw, like Jabba the Hutt on steroids. Huge, mean, and full of hate.

At various points over the years, Gina and I would try to reach out to her.

"Mom, don't you want to see your grandchildren? Frankie and Christina are growing up so fast, and they ask about you."

No response.

Well, actually, there were two responses. One was that occasionally she'd be friendly, since she'd come up with a new way of trying to swindle money from us. The other response was unbridled hostility. I'd talk with her about what an incredibly liberating thing it had been for me to find out that God was real and that we could have a relationship with Him. I wanted the opportunity to ask her forgiveness for any wrongs I'd done to her.

She'd put up her hand. "F— you! Take your Bible and shove it up yourself! Go to h—!"

I never did figure out why she was telling me to go to hell when she believed that there was no such place.

Trying to connect with my mother meant stepping into a whirlpool of pain. She had no regrets about her deceit, no repentance about the awful choices she'd made, and no concern about the ways she wounded me as a kid. So there it was. No happy ending, no great reconciliation or restoration. My mother had no interest in a relationship with me, Gina, or our children.

I had two choices. I could deny how much that hurt, stuff it inside, and limp along as if all was well—I hated facades, as you know, so this wasn't an option—or I could acknowledge the pain and learn to live with it. I decided that I wouldn't use my mom's wrongs as an offensive weapon against her. I wouldn't hover nearby, wanting revenge and trying to hurt her with the ugly facts of how much she'd hurt me. I didn't excuse my mother's choices, but I also knew that the ultimate enemy in this was Satan. The Bible says he loves to destroy lives; in fact, he is described as a hungry lion, looking for people to devour. He'd done that to my mom, leaving her as a grotesque parody of a person. But I wasn't going to let dark feelings against my mom destroy *my* life. This is where I had to draw deep into the reality

of who Jesus really is and the fact that He is truly stronger than Satan.
Jesus could take what was meant for evil and use it for good.

As I said, my dad somehow continued to live with my mother in
their apartment in Upland. He'd come to our house about once a
month for dinner. I wish I could say that we recouped our lost years
and developed a deep, strong relationship . . . but we just didn't have
a way to talk with each other about anything beyond the surface.

I brought up Christ many times, but he wasn't interested in making a decision to connect with Jesus. He was uncomfortable if I
brought up my feelings. So I'd ask him open-ended questions about
his life: "Dad, what was the war like for you?" "Tell me about the
coolest building you ever built." "Hey, what did you like best when
you were playing baseball in the minors?"

Maybe it was partly the generation he came from and partly his
own dysfunction, but he'd just give one- or two-word answers. So we
kept it simple, and our kids got to know their granddad a little bit,
and that was good.

Then one day when I hadn't talked with my dad for a few weeks,
we got a call from my mother. I hadn't seen her for several years.

"Frankie, this is your mother. Your father had a stroke, and he's
in the hospital. He doesn't have much time."

Click.

I rushed to the hospital. My dad was paralyzed. A few days later
they moved him into a convalescent home. He couldn't talk, except
to say one thing, over and over: "Oh, s—!" Anything else he tried to
say came out backward. His brain circuits were scrambled. He could
understand what we were saying to him, but he couldn't say anything
coherent to us.

But then a miracle happened.

My dad's brother had recently married a wonderful woman named Arnetta, and they came to visit Dad in the hospital. Arnetta talked to Dad about Jesus. He listened. She asked him if he wanted to receive Jesus. He did. And then, somehow, he put two words together that she could understand: "Tell Frankie!"

That was the last thing my dad ever said. He died the next day.

Mother told us she wouldn't come to the funeral. She said she didn't have any shoes to wear.

Gina and I went over to my parents' apartment. Mom was going to pitch Dad's stuff, and I wanted to gather up pieces of his life. We brought the kids, whom Mom hadn't seen in years.

"My," she said to our son, Frankie, "you're a big, tall guy, aren't you? I hope you're not gonna grow up to be a bum like your dad!"

Frankie didn't know what to say. He and Gina and Christina left for a while, and I went through my father's photos—of a young military man in Korea . . . smiling with his buddies from the union . . . wearing his uniform on the baseball field.

There was one picture I loved the most: my dad, with his big, bright smile, standing next to the wall of Memorial Park in Upland. The ball field there had put up a plaque in his honor years before. "*In tribute to Frank Pastore,*" it said, "*whose untiring devotion to this ball field and those who play here will be an everlasting inspiration to us all.*" In the picture, my dad looked a little shy about standing next to this sign that honored him, but he was beaming.

Crying like a crazy man, I set the photo aside so I could take it home to get a frame for it.

My dad also had memory boxes. During World War II, he'd served with the U.S. Army Corps of Engineers, building radio towers and big steel bridges. He'd never told me much about that. But here were his medals . . . and here was his watch, an old gold Hamilton inscribed *"To Frank from Mother and Dad, Christmas, 1950."* I wear that watch to this day.

In the closet were Dad's letterman jackets from high school, when he was a shot-putter, and baseball jackets from his days playing semi-pro. There was also a giant stack of mint-condition *Playboy* magazines. I wasn't quite sure what to do with those. I didn't want to throw them away; after all, they were a tangible link with my dad, who was gone. But they weren't exactly a keepsake. I thought briefly about selling them on eBay and donating the proceeds to ministry, in my dad's name. But that didn't seem quite right either. So I threw them away.

When we got home, I gave Gina the photo of Dad for framing. Our house was a zoo, with guests coming and going, and Gina stuck the photo in a magazine for safekeeping. Then, in between guests, Mrs. Pignotti cleaned up. She threw away the magazines. The garbage truck came. My dad's photo was gone.

Gina was sick about this chain of events, and in my distressed state, I was a basket case. At the funeral, I was weeping, talking about the lost photo that had so perfectly captured my dad's grin.

Then my niece Lizzy waved something in the air. It was an 8-by-10 photo.

"You mean this one?" she yelled.

Somehow Lizzy, daughter of my half sister, whom I'd seen only six times in my life, had ended up with a copy of my dad's photo with his plaque.

I wept harder. "Yes!"

After my dad's death, my mother continued to "live" in her apartment in Upland. I never saw her. Didn't want to. It was too toxic. Too difficult. Too painful. Gina and I reached out occasionally by phone, but there was no change in my mother's desire to have a relationship with any of us. She would just hang up. Then one day I got a call from my half sister.

"Frank," she said, "this is your sister, Lynn."

"Hi, Lynn," I said. "How are you?"

"Well, Frank, it's about Mom. She's not doing well. I don't think she has much time left. If you want to see her before she passes, you'd better come."

Lynn had been as wounded by our mother as I had been. She understood when I told her I wasn't sure quite what to do. I thanked her for the update and hung up. I was getting ready to leave for a speaking engagement out of town, and as I thought about the right thing to do, I honestly felt no compulsion or leading to go see my mom.

I went to the speaking engagement.

I had another call from Lynn. "Mom has passed," she said.

"Lynn," I told her, "I'm sorry to say this, but I know you'll understand. Mom died to me years ago."

★   ★   ★

Everyone wants great relationships with their parents. We all wish we had wonderful memories of security, love, and nurture. As you can tell from my story, I mourn the loss of what could have been with my dad. I don't know why he didn't connect with me more and override my mother's evil influence. I don't know why I didn't reach out to him more. When I think about losing him, I feel deep pain. When I think about my mother, I feel deep anger.

I wish the story could have been different. I wish I could tell you that it was all resolved, that faith in Jesus has solved—in a way I could see in this life—all the problems and confusion of my experience with my parents. But that wouldn't be real.

I believe that God can do miracles. But often He allows broken things to remain broken in this life, and we can't figure out why.

But one aspect of all this has been mended. After I came to know Christ, I realized that I couldn't change my past, but I could, by God's power, change the choices I made in the present. I could change the legacy my kids grew up with. I might have had a passive dad and a mean mom and a godless childhood, but that didn't have to be the case for my son and daughter. By God's mercy, the generational chains could be broken, and our kids could grow up with a legacy of grace.

Some people who aren't parents may think they know exactly how to raise perfect children. But those of us who are parents know how hard it is. Nothing has shown me my own sin, my own brokenness, like being a husband and a father. But these roles have also shown me—in a way nothing else could—the unbelievable extent of God's tender ability to redeem and make new. In my relationship with Frankie, God redeemed the lost bond I never had with my father. And He made it new in ways that surprised me . . . like the fact that Frankie was just not a baseball fan.

I grew up with the same name as my dad. When Gina gave birth to our son, as he fought to live in his first hours, we gave him my name. Once Frankie grew and became strong, I had fond dreams that he and I would play catch in the yard, just like me and my dad. I dreamed of him following me to the big leagues. I knew it would all be wonderful.

From the time Frankie was tiny, I'd sit on the floor with him, rolling a big ball to him. He hated it. As he got older we'd play catch, and he'd be asking from the very beginning, "Can we stop now?"

He didn't like going to the ballpark; the fireworks—or "fire pops" as he called them—scared him. Eventually he got over that, but all he wanted to do at the park was eat hot dogs. I was befuddled. All my friends' sons were little clones of their fathers. They loved baseball. My son didn't.

I started to realize I needed to connect with Frankie in areas *he* enjoyed. He loved driving Tonka trucks, so I'd let him sit next to me and shift gears while I drove my Porsche. *Do not try this at home!*

I'd let him drive the golf cart when I played golf, and he loved that. Meanwhile, ever the jock, I was thinking, "Come on, kid. When are you gonna pick up a club?" But no, he was content to just drive the cart . . . until he was about 14.

Then Frankie tried out for the school golf team. I ran out and bought him his own set of clubs. I'd work with him; after all, I was a pitching coach, right? I should be able to coach golf as well. I did, but he learned best from Gina's dad. And soon Frankie was beating me. Regularly.

The differences between us weren't just in sports. Frankie is musically gifted and became an incredible pianist. I have no musical ability. In school Frankie was brilliant in math and science but didn't care a hoot about philosophy or history, the very disciplines that turn me on. Frankie is rather quiet; I am verbal.

Like most dads I have regrets about my parenting. I'm sad that I was so busy with "ministry" during my Talbot days that I didn't spend more time with my kids. I wish I had learned earlier in their lives that you absolutely have to schedule your kids' events into your calendar, or you'll miss the things that are important to them.

But I can look back and say that by God's grace, Frankie and Christina grew up with a different dad and mom than Gina and I did.

They grew up in a home where the grace of God covered a multitude of sins. They saw reconciliation and forgiveness and real, deep love every day.

They would be the first to tell you that we're not perfect and they aren't either. But they would also say that the generational curse was broken. Because of the love of God, I didn't have to be the same kind of parent that my parents were to me. And because of the love of God, we love each other more than I ever could have dreamed was possible. Our home became a home of blessing rather than curses.

As I write, Christina is launched in her career as a successful cos-motologist. Frankie and his wonderful wife, Jessica, have established their own home in Southern California. Frankie isn't a professional athlete or a talk-show host. He went to dental school at UCLA. So he's a dentist. A great dentist.

And as I write, Jessica just gave birth to their firstborn. A boy. Michael John Pastore. My grandson. You know me well enough by now to know I'm crying as I write these words. And here's the mira-cle that makes me weep: I may have grown up with loss and pain. It may never have been "fixed" in this life. But I didn't have to carry those curses into my son's life. By God's grace, those chains were bro-ken. And now Michael Pastore, all eight pounds of him, can look forward to blessings rather than curses, to a future and a hope.

38

★ ★ ★

AT PEACE WITH THE PIECES

I wrote this book because people need the Lord. I know that sounds trite, but it's true. I grew up as an evolutionist, an atheist, and a relativist with a dysfunctional family. I can relate to how nonbelievers view Christianity. I really hated how naive, gullible, and reactionary Christians seemed to be.

I had fragments of information; you know, like people today who have a little science here, a little New Age mysticism there, a little secular skepticism mixed with the latest life expert on *Oprah*. All those TV documentaries on why Christianity and the Bible are so antiscience didn't help much. Neither did movies in which Christians are always either the twisted, nutcase killer at worst or the fat, irrelevant weirdo at best.

Left to my own devices, I would have continued on my less-than-merry way as an atheist and materialist, always hungry for more, trying without success to satisfy the emptiness inside. But as you know from reading this book, God had other plans for me. Good plans, though they often emerged from brokenness and wreckage. A splintered pitching arm spurred me on a search for God. People who aren't absolutely desperate don't tend to look for Him, so it took the shattering of my identity and career for me to consider the real reasons to believe.

Then I experienced fractured trust in my relationships in Christian ministry, of all places. That betrayal led me on a journey through my broken past that I otherwise wouldn't have taken. It led to deep inner healing I wouldn't have sought out.

For many years I wanted life to look perfect, because then everything would be all right. But it never *was* perfect, of course. Trying to present a nice picture to the outside world was just an exhausting facade, doomed to crumble with time.

Now when I find broken pieces in my day, rather than thinking I'm doing something wrong, not exercising enough faith, not being disciplined enough, not being whatever, I tend to look up beyond myself to consider the bigger picture. Now I find a certain strange pleasure when life is in upheaval. I know that God is on the move.

And now I find that I'm not so driven toward arriving at a certain destination—like attaining professional prominence or achieving financial security. Now I don't feel in such a hurry. Life these days is more about enjoying the journey, because I know that God has assured the destination.

Now, even though I almost hate to say it, I'm at peace with the pieces.

When I was a little boy and my mother took me on a rare road trip back to her home in Alabama, our journey took us along hundreds of miles of Interstate 40 in Texas. There we were, tooling along in the Riviera, my mom chain-smoking and me sitting in the front seat beside her without a seat belt, wearing my powder-blue knit shirt with the yellow stripes, matching blue shorts, and sandals similar to those worn by elderly Florida retirees.

Then the billboards started: FREE STEAK! 140 MILES! FREE STEAK! 120 MILES! FREE STEAK! 100 MILES!

The big signs showed a cowboy with an absolutely enormous cut of beef. I daydreamed for mile after mile about getting to Amarillo, Texas, home of the world-famous Big Texan Steak Ranch, featuring a 72-ounce steak (four and a half pounds!), free for anyone who could eat it in an hour.

My mom, as you know, was all about supersizing me. We got to the Big Texan, and on that first trip even I couldn't attempt an assault on the 72-ounce steak. I had a huge hamburger instead.

About eight or nine years later, in 1976, as a young professional baseball player, I was tooling along I-40 in my 280Z. I saw those roadside signs for the Big Texan and remembered my childhood fascination with the giant steak. I still loved to eat, and now, as a young man paying my own way, the main attraction grabbed me even more: It was *free*!

So I parked my Z and ambled in. The Big Texan hadn't changed its decor since my childhood. The walls were covered with horns and cowhides, spurs, and Texas memorabilia. The waitresses were friendly. It was a manly kind of place. I announced my desire for the free steak.

I was ushered to a special table. A waitress brought out the 72-ouncer, raw, so I could look it over. It was as big as a saddle, but thicker. She asked how I'd like it cooked and informed me that in order to get it free, I needed to also consume a shrimp cocktail, baked potato, dinner salad, roll, and butter, all within an hour. She told me I needed to pay up front because if I didn't quite eat it all and had to pay at the end, I'd be so full I wouldn't be able to reach into my hip pocket to get my wallet. But if I ate it all within 60 minutes, they'd give me my money back.

I didn't even wear a watch back then, but it seemed like a reasonable gamble to me. They cooked my steak, medium rare, brought it out, set a giant timer, and away I went.

I finished the whole shebang in 21 minutes.

They were impressed. The Big Texan world record, held by an eating machine (and professional wrestler) named Klondike Bill, was 20 minutes, and I'd almost beaten him without even knowing what I was doing. I was an instant celebrity . . . an 18-year-old kid in a Cincinnati Reds' jacket, passing through town on my way to spring training in Florida.

So when I was on my way back to California, of course I stopped at the Big Texan again. This time I took down the Steak in 19 minutes.

Klondike Bill was not pleased. Piqued, he ate New Jersey. And then he came down to Amarillo to get his title back. He consumed the Steak in 18 minutes.

Now it was war. I stopped at the Big Texan every time I was on my way to and from spring training. I ate the Steak and all its trimmings in 17 minutes the next time; then 15; then 13; then 11. Then I brought it down to a cool 9.5 minutes.

My record stood for 21 years. My fame as a pitcher may have waxed and waned according to my stats, but at the Big Texan I was golden. The only time my record was beaten was when a guy from Florida brought his 500-pound Bengal tiger to the Big Texan. The tiger cheated: His meal was limited to just the Steak, since tigers aren't big on baked potatoes and the like. He dined outside, in front of the restaurant. His technique was simple: sniff, lick, gulp. The Steak was gone in 90 seconds.

But most of my competitors were human. Even today you can go to the Big Texan's Web site and watch videos of man versus Steak, big guys with their mouths full of beef, drooling red and chowing down on the challenge. Plenty of women have beaten the Steak as well, including a grandmother who wiped her mouth, smiled, and neatly reapplied her lipstick after engulfing four and a half pounds of cow.

You're probably wondering about my technique. It was all in the wrist: I'd cut that bovine slab into as many tiny pieces as I could as fast as I could. Then I'd do a one-chomp, swallow routine, bite by bite by bite.

But records are made to be broken. My day of reckoning came on March 24, 2008. The sky was overcast. Bursts of dry wind blew tumbleweeds in front of the Big Texan as Joey "Jaws" Chestnut pulled into town.

Joey pushed through the doors. Conversation stopped. Strong men's hearts quailed within them.

"I'm here to try the Big Steak!" said Joey.

Joey "Jaws" Chestnut was four years old when I set my best Steak record. Now he's a nice young man who just seems to have this incredible knack for eating ridiculous amounts of food in short amounts of time. He once ate 47 grilled-cheese sandwiches in 10 minutes; 10.5 pounds of macaroni and cheese in 7 minutes; nearly 10 pounds of pork in 12 minutes; 68 hot dogs—with buns—in 10 minutes; 103 hamburgers in 10 minutes. He fasts, stretches his stomach with water, and then engulfs his food victims like a friendly boa constrictor.

That day back in March 2008, Joey took down the 4.5-pound Steak, shrimp cocktail, baked potato, dinner salad, roll, butter, and several paper doilies in 8 minutes 52 seconds.

I was history.

★   ★   ★

I haven't been back to the Big Texan in years. The thrill is gone, I guess. But I smile when I think of my days as a young man, racing across the country, pitching hard, loving the big leagues, chasing after my dreams as fast as I could. There was a time in my life when it was all out in front of me, there for the taking. It wasn't just the Big Steak; I wanted everything, as much as I could have, always a little bit more, almost as if I was trying to satisfy some hunger inside that had driven me crazy ever since I was a kid.

Maybe that Big Steak was really a metaphor . . . and so I didn't mind my eating record being shattered. It was a funny reminder of a time gone by. But now I've finally realized I don't need more. I don't feel like I have to gulp life down, always hungry for more.

No, now I'm free to take my time and savor every bite of life, the bitter with the sweet—and yes, even those pieces that are shattered—because I know I'm in God's hands.

AFTERWORD

Many early *Shattered* readers asked for a "where are they now" update about both the Pignotti family and my baseball buddies. Here's where they are now.

Gina's dad, John—Dad Pignotti—passed away on December 28, 2006. He died of vascular dementia at the age of 77. He was loved by many; more than seven hundred people showed up for his funeral. Gina's mom, Ann, still lives in Upland, right around the corner from Gina and me, and is surrounded by family and friends.

Gina's only sister, Marina, lives in a nearby town with her husband, and has been blessed with four grandchildren. Gina's brother Johnny lives in Scottsdale with his wife, Staci. Their two daughters live in Tucson, where their eldest daughter just gave them their first grandson. Gina's youngest brother, Nick, lives in Southern California with his wife, Janelle, and their three children.

★ ★ ★

Regarding Tommy Hume, Tom Foley, Duane Walker, and Dann Bilardello: They eventually moved on from the Reds via trades and releases. Tommy Hume retired as a player in 1987, but went on to be the Reds' bullpen coach from 1996 through 2007. Tom Foley retired as a player in 1995, but today is the third-base coach for the Tampa Bay Rays. Duane Walker retired as a player in 1988; Dann Bilardello retired as a player in 1992, but is a minor-league manager today. I haven't had contact with these guys in years, but I remain forever grateful for their roles in my life.

FOCUS ON THE FAMILY®

Welcome to the Family —

Whether you purchased this book, borrowed it, or received it as a gift, we're glad you're reading it. It's just one of the many helpful, encouraging, and biblically based resources produced by Focus on the Family® for people in all stages of life.

Focus began in 1977 with the vision of one man, Dr. James Dobson, a licensed psychologist and author of numerous best-selling books on marriage, parenting, and family. Alarmed by the societal, political, and economic pressures that were threatening the existence of the American family, Dr. Dobson founded Focus on the Family with one employee and a once-a-week radio broadcast aired on 36 stations.

Now an international organization reaching millions of people daily, Focus on the Family is dedicated to preserving values and strengthening and encouraging families through the life-changing message of Jesus Christ.

Focus on the Family MAGAZINES

These faith-building, character-developing publications address the interests, issues, concerns, and challenges faced by every member of your family from preschool through the senior years.

For More INFORMATION

ONLINE:
Log on to
FocusOnTheFamily.com
In Canada, log on to
FocusOnTheFamily.ca

PHONE:
Call toll-free:
800-A-FAMILY
(232-6459)
In Canada, call toll-free:
800-661-9800

| FOCUS ON THE FAMILY THRIVING FAMILY™ Marriage & parenting | FOCUS ON THE FAMILY CLUBHOUSE JR.™ Ages 4 to 8 | FOCUS ON THE FAMILY CLUBHOUSE® Ages 8 to 12 | FOCUS ON THE FAMILY CITIZEN® U.S. news issues |

Rev. 10/09

More Great Resources
from Focus on the Family®

Pete Maravich
The Authorized Biography of Pistol Pete
Wayne Federman and Marshall Terrill in collaboration with Jackie Maravich
Pete Maravich became a basketball legend at LSU and subsequently was named one of the top 50 players in NBA history. But "Pistol" Pete's success on the court often masked emotional pain. Pete's life changed when he came to faith in God. At 40 Pete Maravich died tragically. After two decades of silence, Jackie Maravich has welcomed authors Wayne Federman and Marshall Terrill into Pete's private world, granting unprecedented access for this authorized biography.

Championship Fathering
How to Win at Being a Dad
by Carey Casey with Neil Wilson
Championship fathers aren't perfect. They just keep practicing the three fundamentals of being an effective dad: *loving, coaching,* and *modeling.* That takes a game plan, and Carey Casey's got it. Whether you're a fatherhood rookie or a field-battered veteran, this practical, inspiring guide will turn the business of being a dad into one of your greatest pleasures.

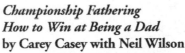

Castaway Kid
One Man's Search for Hope and Home
by R.B. Mitchell
Castaway Kid is the real-life story of a child abandoned in an orphanage, one of the last in America. As a young man, he was on an emotional roller coaster of bitterness . . . until finding his home and hope in knowing God.

FOR MORE INFORMATION

Online:
Log on to FocusOnTheFamily.com
In Canada, log on to focusonthefamily.ca.

Phone:
Call toll free: 800-A-FAMILY
In Canada, call toll free: 800-661-9800.

BPZZXP